Teacher's Annotated Edition

Mathematics Workshop

Problem Solving 1

Globe Book Company, Inc.
Englewood Cliffs, New Jersey

Consultant

Dr. Alan Barson

Director, Chapter 1 Secondary Mathematics Program
City of Philadelphia
Philadelphia, Pennsylvania

Developed and produced for Globe Book Company by

Publicom, Inc.

ISBN: 1-55675-901-0 (Teacher's Annotated Edition)

PRINTED IN THE UNITED STATES OF AMERICA   2 3 4 5 6 7 8 9 0

To The Teacher

Problem Solving 1 and *Problem Solving 2* are part of the **Globe Mathematics Workshop** series. These two books are designed expressly to help students who are experiencing difficulty in problem solving in mathematics.

Difficulties in solving word problems rest largely in the areas of using reading skills and applying critical thinking skills.

Reading Skills: The instructional paragraphs and the problems in these two books are written at a controlled reading level, one that is well within the capabilities of most junior high school students achieving below grade level. Every new instructional concept is accompanied by an example, providing the student with an immediate application of the skill. In addition, the subject matter of the problems has been carefully selected to relate to students' everyday experiences. From the outset, students constantly use and check their reading comprehension skills. After reading each problem, they identify the question(s) being asked and then restate the question(s) in their own words.

Critical Thinking Skills: In following the problem solving steps outlined in these books, students come to develop and use both intellectual and decision-making critical thinking skills. *Intellectual skills,* such as classifying, interpreting, analyzing, summarizing, synthesizing, and evaluating information, are all used in finding information and selecting the relevant facts needed to solve a problem. *Decision-making skills* are used in eliminating nonrelevant information, in determining the correct mathematics operations, and in selecting the most suitable strategy (or strategies) for solving the problem.

Problem Solving 1 and *Problem Solving 2* may be used to supplement the problem solving sections of any basal mathematics program. They may also be used as a "stand-alone" program—either for students achieving below grade level or as a review of problem solving techniques for students of average ability.

Problem Solving 1 and Problem Solving 2

The two books in this series are self-contained. In *Problem Solving 1,* the pace of content coverage is carefully controlled, with considerable time devoted to cumulative practice of newly introduced skills and strategies.

Problem Solving 2 reintroduces and reinforces the problem solving skills and strategies developed in Book 1 at a faster pace and with new practice problems. Additional skills and strategies are introduced and applied to problems of a more complex nature. Book 2 concludes with the application of problem solving skills and strategies to problems that are found in practical, day-to-day situations.

The Five-Step Process

In *Problem Solving 1* and *Problem Solving 2,* the approach to solving all word problems is based on a five-step model. The "steps" in this model are as follows:

1. **Read the problem.** This first step helps the student to separate a problem into its two main parts—information and *the question being asked.* The ability to restate the question in a different form indicates that the student has identified and understood the question.

2. **Find the facts.** Once the question has been identified and understood, the student must decide what facts are needed to answer the question. The needed facts may be found "inside" or "outside" of the question. In some instances, the needed facts may not be obtainable, in which case that problem cannot be solved.

3. **Plan what to do.** At this step, the student must decide what strategy to use in order to answer the question. If an estimate of the answer can be made, it is made at this time.

4. **Carry out the plan.** This step represents the execution of the plan. It may be simply to perform one or more mathematics operations (addition, subtraction, multiplication, division), or it may be a *nonroutine* strategy.

5. **Check the answer.** Once a solution to a problem has been reached, it is critically examined during this step for reasonableness and accuracy.

In *Problem Solving 1,* this approach to problem solving is developed step-by-step until the entire model is complete. Thereafter, the model serves as a consistent framework for solving any word problem.

It is understood that many simple problems can be solved without going through all the steps of the model. However, students are encouraged to complete each discrete step, in order, for *every* problem they are asked to solve, regardless of its degree of difficulty. Such a disciplined approach to problem solving helps to reduce or eliminate the errors of omission or commission that so often occur as a result of hasty or disorganized problem solving techniques.

Organization and Features of the Books

Units

The content material in each book is divided into units. Book 1 is divided into three units based on the following: understanding the five-step model, developing the problem solving skills at each step, and learning more about problem solving strategies.

Book 2 is divided into four units. The first three units cover much of the same material as Units 1–3 of Book 1. However, Unit 1 is a *review* of the five-step model, while Units 2 and 3 *reinforce* and *extend* the skills and strategies developed in those same units in Book 1. Unit 4 deals with *applications* of problem solving skills and strategies to such everyday situations as balancing checkbooks and computing sales taxes.

Lessons

Each instructional lesson in these books is two pages in length and has an identical format. The format for each lesson is as follows:

> *Aim:* This is a statement of the goal or objective of the lesson.

> *What You Need to Know:* This section contains all of the information needed to reach the objective of the lesson.

> *Think About It:* This section serves several purposes. First, it asks the student to answer one or two questions about the *What You Need to Know* section, "forcing" the student to stop and think about what was just read. This is followed by one or two Examples that apply or illustrate the point of the lesson. Usually in the form of sample problems, these Examples prepare the student for the *Practice* problems coming up. Concise explanations follow the Examples, helping to ensure that the student has understood the application of the lesson concept.

> *Practice:* This section consists of several practice problems. These problems are similar to the samples used in the *Think About It* Examples.

The consistency of lesson length and format helps students become more comfortable with the content material. The fact that their responsibilities in each lesson are predictable makes the content seem less threatening.

Unit Reviews

Each unit is followed by a three-page *Unit Review*. Each *Unit Review* contains a variety of exercise types: true-false, sentence-completion, and multiple-choice items as well as problems for which the student demonstrates the use of all five problem solving steps in writing.

Additional Practice

For each lesson in the book, this section has a corresponding page of practice exercises. The page number is given at the end of each lesson in the student edition.

The exercises in this section provide flexibility to the program in that they can be utilized in a variety of ways. For example, they may be used as additional classroom work, as homework assignments, as extra credit or enrichment, or as evaluation aids. The way in which these exercises are used depends, to a large degree, on the ability of the students in your class and the pace at which they proceed through lessons.

Whole-Book Review

Each book in this series concludes with a *Whole-Book Review*. Problems in the *Whole-Book Review* are of the exercise type that concludes each *Unit Review,* namely, the type that requires the student actually to demonstrate his or her thinking during each of the five steps in the problem solving process. This review is designed to help you to evaluate student mastery of all the skills and concepts developed in the book.

Appendix

Each book has an *Appendix.* Obtaining information from an appendix is one of the skills developed in the course of this program. Thus, students will be required to refer to the *Appendix* in order to solve certain problems in each book.

Teaching the Lessons

Depending on your students' level of achievement, most of the lessons in these books may be completed in a single class period (not including the *Additional Practice* exercises). The following is one possible "timetable" for teaching the lessons in these books.

1. Read the lesson *Aim,* or have a student read it. Be sure that everyone understands what the lesson is about.

2. Lead students through the *What You Need to Know* section. Take as much time as necessary with this section. It contains the essential content of the lesson.

3. Have students read the question portion of the *Think About It* section. Once it has been determined that everyone understands the question(s), give students a few minutes to write their answer(s) to the question(s). Have students read their answers.

Proceed to the Example(s) and the explanatory material that follows. Again, make sure that students understand what was done and why. The Examples are models of the exercises in the *Practice* section.

4. Have students start working on the exercises in the *Practice* section. Depending on your students' abilities and pace, you may have them—

a. complete the practice exercises, read their responses aloud, and discuss any questions. You may wish to assign problems from the *Additional Practice* page for homework.

b. work on the exercises until the end of the period and complete the *Practice* section for homework.

5. The next class period should begin with a review of the previous lesson. For more able students, this review may consist of going over the homework assignment. For students working at a slower pace, you may wish to spend the entire period going over the lesson, discussing homework, and working in class on problems from the *Additional Practice* page.

Using the Teacher's Annotations

In the Teacher's Annotated Editions of *Problem Solving 1* and *Problem Solving 2,* annotations are printed, in color, directly on the student pages. These annotations consist of the following:

Answers or responses to questions   In many cases, these consist of "suggested" or "acceptable" responses, since more than one correct response is frequently possible.

Teaching hints and suggestions   These consist of background information, alternative approaches to problems, suggested items for class discussion, and particular "trouble items" to watch for—items that frequently prove difficult for students.

As noted above, these annotations appear on the student pages in the Teacher's Annotated Editions; thus the information is available when and where it is needed.

A Note About Calculators
The use of hand-held calculators in the mathematics classroom is becoming widespread. In some schools, the use of calculators is required. Many of the exercises in these books lend themselves readily to the use of calculators. At numerous points throughout the Teacher's Annotated Editions, the suggested use of the calculator as a computational tool is offered as an annotation. Students learn that there are times when the execution of a plan is best done mentally or using paper and pencil, and there are times when the execution is best done with a calculator.

Mathematics Workshop

Problem Solving 1

Globe Book Company, Inc.
Englewood Cliffs, New Jersey

Consultant

Dr. Alan Barson

Director, Chapter 1 Secondary Mathematics Program
City of Philadelphia
Philadelphia, Pennsylvania

Developed and produced for Globe Book Company by

Publicom, Inc.

Art and Photography Credits:

The illustrations were prepared by Judy Love.

The photographs were obtained from the following sources: Janice Fullman/The Picture Cube, p. 1; Andrew Brilliant, p. 23; Frank Siteman/ The Picture Cube, p. 53

Cover photo—Andrew Brilliant and Carol Palmer.

ISBN: 1-55675-901-0 (Teacher's Annotated Edition)
ISBN: 1-55675-900-2 (Student Edition)

PRINTED IN THE UNITED STATES OF AMERICA   2 3 4 5 6 7 8 9 0

Contents

Introductory Lesson

Aim: To learn how lessons are organized in this book, and to start thinking about word problems

What You Need to Know

Mathematics Workshop: Problem Solving 1 has three units. In the first unit, you will learn the five basic steps for solving word problems. In the second and third units, you will apply these steps to different types of problems. By the time you finish this book, you will own many "keys" for solving word problems.

Every lesson in this book starts with an "Aim," just as this lesson does. Each lesson is organized into three parts: "What You Need to Know," "Think About It," and "Practice."

The "What You Need to Know" section describes the main ideas for the lesson.

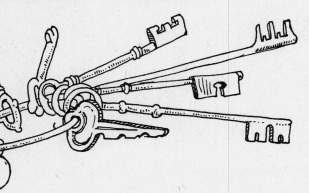

Think About It

The "Think About It" section asks you to answer a question. The question relates to what you just read in "What You Need to Know."

How many basic steps are there for solving word problems?

There are five basic steps.

Next, the "Think About It" section gives you one or more "Examples" to study. The Examples give you a way of looking at what you have learned so far.

Suppose the "What You Need to Know" section in this lesson talked about the five steps for solving word problems. Then the Example might be like the one shown on the next page. It shows how the five steps work for a given word problem. (This is the longest Example you will find in the whole book!)

Example Students sold 175 tickets for the class play. The tickets cost $2.50 each. How much money did the students collect?

Step 1: READ and REREAD the problem; REWORD the question.
What amount of money was collected?

Step 2: FIND the needed facts.
Cost of a ticket: $2.50   Number sold: 175

Step 3: PLAN what to do.
Multiply: number of tickets sold × price of one ticket = total amount collected

Step 4: CARRY OUT the plan.

2.50
× 175
437.50   Answer: $437.50

Step 5: CHECK the answer.
Multiply the other way:

175
× 2.50
437.50

or

Divide:

$$175 \overline{)437.50}$$ 2.50

The Example is used here for two reasons: (1) It shows you how detailed an Example is. (2) It gives you a general idea of what the rest of this book will be about.

Following the Examples in a lesson is a paragraph like the one above. It is a brief statement about the Examples.

Practice

Finally, you come to the third part of the lesson. It is the "Practice" section. Now you will show how well you have understood the information in the lesson. If you have trouble with the Practice items, reread the "What You Need to Know" section and study the Examples again.

1. How many units are in this book? 3 _____

2. What does each lesson start with? an "Aim" _____

3. How many sections are in a lesson? 3 _____

4. What part of a lesson shows how information is applied to a specific situation?

   the "Example" _____

5. Read this word problem:

   Act 1 of the class play is 35 minutes. Act 2 is 23 minutes. There is a 15-minute intermission between acts. How long is it from the beginning to the end of the play?

   Write the number of the step that each of the following represents for the problem.

   a. Step __3__: Add: Act 1 minutes + Act 2 minutes + intermission minutes = total minutes

   b. Step __1__: How many minutes is it from the start of Act 1 to the end of Act 2?

   c. Either Step __4__ or Step __5__: 35 + 23 + 15 = 73

At the end of each unit is a three-page "Unit Review." Look at the Unit 1 Review on pages 20–22 to see how it is organized. At the end of the book are —

- Additional Practice items for each lesson (pages 83–117)
- Whole-Book Review (pages 118–120)
- Appendix (pages 121–122)

Take a look at these sections now.

Mathematics Workshop: Problem Solving 1 has a simple organization. It will make it simpler for you to unlock your own word problems.

1 Five Steps For Solving Problems

- Step One: Read the Problem
- Step Two: Find the Facts
- Cumulative Practice: Steps 1 and 2
- Step Three: Plan What to Do
- Cumulative Practice: Steps 1, 2, and 3
- Step Four: Carry Out the Plan
- Cumulative Practice: Steps 1, 2, 3, and 4
- Step Five: Check the Answer
- Cumulative Practice: Steps 1, 2, 3, 4, and 5

Step One: Read the Problem

Aim: To read a word problem and reword the question

What You Need to Know

Word problems can be divided into two basic parts — information and questions. Before you can begin to solve any word problem, you must first *understand the question* you are being asked to answer. Thus, the first step in solving any word problem is to—

- READ the problem all the way through,
- REREAD the problem more slowly, and
- REWORD the question.

This step is just as simple as it sounds. It is also very important. A common mistake is to "short-cut" this first step. Don't start trying to solve a word problem until you *understand the question.*

If you're 13 and your brother's 3 years younger, how old is he?

That's easy! I'm 3 years older than my brother.

Think About It

The first step in solving a word problem has three parts. What are these parts?

Read the problem all the way through, reread the problem more slowly,

and reword the question.

Read the following word problems. Notice how the question is restated in Example A and reworded in Example B.

Example A For a class play, the students need 14 costumes. They have made 9 costumes. How many more costumes do they have to make?

The Question: *How many more costumes do they have to make?*

Example B Josh was 8 minutes early for rehearsal. Chris was 6 minutes late. How much later to rehearsal was Chris than Josh?

The Question: *How many minutes after Josh arrived did Chris arrive?*

In Example A, the question is restated exactly as it appears in the word problem. In Example B, the question is **reworded.**

Rewording the question in a word problem is a good way to check that you understand the question. If you can reword the question, even slightly, then you have understood the words in the problem. You know exactly what you need to find out.

Teacher Note: Accept any degree of rewording as long as some amount of rewording has occurred while retaining the meaning. Although students are not asked to solve the Practice problems, many students will do so. Answers to the problems are included for your information.

Practice

Reword the question in each of the following word problems. Some questions can be reworded more completely than other questions.

1. There are 23 students painting scenery for the play. Each student paints for 4 hours. How long will it take to paint the scenery?

   The Question: How many hours will it take to paint the scenery?

   _____

                                                    (92 hours)

2. The students are planning to set up 250 chairs for the audience. They have already set up 175 chairs. What number of chairs still need to be set up for everyone to have a seat?

   The Question: How many more chairs still need to be set up?

   _____

                                                    (75 chairs)

3. Ms. Ritter's class sold 54 tickets, Mr. Grant's class sold 47 tickets, and Mrs. Garcia's class sold 62 tickets. What is the total number of tickets that were sold by all three classes?

   The Question: How many tickets were sold in all?

   _____

                                                    (163 tickets)

4. Diane's part has 22 lines in the play. Rod's part has 53 lines. How many more lines does Rod have to learn than Diane has to learn?

   The Question: What is the difference in the number of lines Diane and

   Rod have to learn?   (31 lines)

5. James spent 30 minutes a day for 5 days learning his lines. Sissy spent 15 minutes a day for 8 days learning her lines. What was the difference in the amount of time the two students spent learning lines?

   The Question: How much more time did one student spend learning

   lines than the other student spent?   (30 minutes)

Additional word problems for Lesson 1 skills practice are on page 83.

3

Step Two: Find the Facts

Aim: To find the facts needed to solve a word problem

What You Need to Know

Remember the two basic parts of any word problem — information and a question. In Step 1, you reworded the question to make sure you understood it. In Step 2, you will go to the information part of the problem. You must FIND THE FACTS you need to solve the problem.

Ask yourself: "What facts, or data, do I *need* in order to find the answer to the question?" Next, read the problem again. This time, look for the facts that are given. Decide which facts you need. In many cases, all the facts are included as part of the problem. Sometimes you will have to go "outside" the problem. You may need to look at a map, a graph, a table, a drawing, or an appendix.

Remember, always keep in mind the *question* you are trying to answer. This will help you to find the needed facts.

Think About It

Name a numerical fact that you might find on a map.

Students may mention longitude/latitude, distance, etc.

Facts are facts are facts. It doesn't really matter where the facts are, as long as you can recognize them when you see them. Read each problem below. Notice where the facts are for each.

Example A The class printed 225 adult tickets and 245 student tickets. How many tickets were printed in all?

The Facts: *Number of adult tickets: 225*
Number of student tickets: 245

Example B The Wong family bought 3 adult tickets. How much did they pay for these tickets?

The Facts: *Cost of an adult ticket: $2.50*
Number of tickets bought: 3

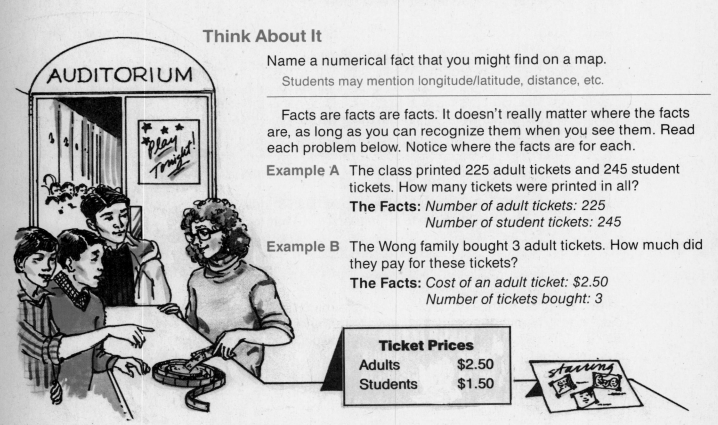

Ticket Prices	
Adults	$2.50
Students	$1.50

In Example A, all the facts are found in the problem. In Example B, only one of the needed facts is found in the problem. The other needed fact is found in a table.

Practice

Write only the facts you need to solve each word problem. Use the information in the word problem. Use the table if you need it.

1. The Bernards bought 6 student tickets. How much money did the Bernards spend?

   The Facts: Number of student tickets: 6
   _____

   Cost of a student ticket: $1.50   ($9.00)
   _____

2. There are 12 student ushers for the play. Seven ushers are from Ms. Ritter's class. The rest are from Mr. Grant's class. How many ushers are from Mr. Grant's class?

   The Facts: Total number of student ushers: 12
   _____

   Number from Ms. Ritter's class: 7   (5 ushers)
   _____

3. The class printed 540 programs. An equal number are given to 12 ushers. How many programs does each usher have?

   The Facts: Total number of programs: 540
   _____

   Number of ushers: 12   (45 programs)
   _____

4. Act 1 in the play takes 35 minutes. Act 2 takes 45 minutes. If the two-act play lasts 95 minutes, how long is intermission?

   The Facts: Total time for play: 95 minutes
   _____

   Time for Act 1: 35 minutes
   _____

   Time for Act 2: 45 minutes   (15 minutes)
   _____

5. The Burns family bought 4 adult tickets. The Martin family bought 2 adult tickets. How much more did the Burns family pay for tickets than the Martin family paid?

   The Facts: Burns family adult tickets: 4
   _____

   Martin family adult tickets: 2
   _____

   Cost of an adult ticket: $2.50   ($5.00)
   _____

Additional word problems for Lesson 2 skills practice are on page 84.

Cumulative Practice: Steps 1 and 2

Aim: To practice with Steps 1 and 2 in combination

What You Need to Know

Now you will think about *both* Steps 1 and 2 as you get ready to solve word problems. Remember, in Step 1, you first READ the problem all the way through. Then you REREAD for details. Look for the key sentence that asks the question. Finally, REWORD the question. Ask it in a different way.

In Step 2, you FIND THE FACTS needed to answer the key question. Focus on only the *important* information in the problem. Remember, all the facts you need may not be "inside" the problem. Think about where you might look "outside" the problem to find them.

Think About It

Name the first two steps in solving a word problem. (Remember, Step 1 has three parts.)

Step 1: Read the problem, reread for details, and reword the question.

_____

Step 2: Find the facts needed to answer the question.

Read each word problem below. The question is underlined. The important facts are circled.

Example A Calvin and Bob have been playing on the school tennis team for 2 years. They won (16 matches) in September and (24 matches) in October. <u>How many matches did they win during September and October?</u>

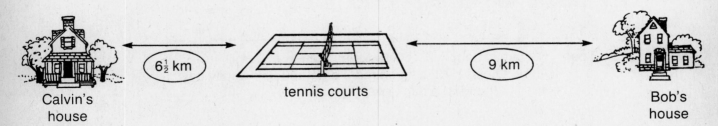

Calvin's house   6½ km   tennis courts   9 km   Bob's house

Example B Every day, Calvin and Bob rode their bikes from their homes to the tennis courts. <u>How much farther did Bob ride to get to the tennis courts than Calvin?</u>

6

In Example A, all the important data are "inside" the problem. In Example B, you must look at the diagram "outside" the problem to find the needed data, or facts.

Practice

For each word problem below, underline the question. Circle the facts needed to solve the problem. Be sure to circle only the important data.

1. On Monday, Betty practiced her forehand for 25 minutes and her backhand for 15 minutes. How many minutes did she spend practicing both her forehand and her backhand? (40 minutes)

2. During a recent tennis match, Wilson served the ball 46 times. Sheila served the ball 49 times. The ball went out of bounds on 11 of these serves. How many more times did Sheila serve the ball than Wilson? (3 more times)

3. After practice, Adam gathered up 15 tennis balls. He put them back in the cans. If he put 3 balls in each can, how many cans did he use? (5 cans)

Tennis Balls
Bounce-Rite $2.25
Smash-Um $1.95
No-Let $2.50

Sale

4. Louis bought 2 cans of Bounce-Rite tennis balls and 3 cans of Smash-Um tennis balls. How much did he pay for the Bounce-Rite balls? ($4.50)

5. Fred lives 4 blocks from the tennis courts. Helen lives $7\frac{1}{2}$ blocks from the tennis courts. They each make a round trip from their own house to the tennis courts. How much farther does Helen walk than Fred? (7 blocks)

Additional word problems for Lesson 3 skills practice are on page 85.

Step Three: Plan What to Do

Aim: To plan how to solve a word problem and, when possible, to estimate the answer

What You Need to Know

Once you understand the question and find the needed facts, you are ready to PLAN WHAT TO DO. You need to **visualize** the problem. Form a picture in your mind of what is going on. This will help you to decide on a "plan of attack."

Often, you will only need to add, subtract, multiply, or divide. Sometimes you will need another **strategy,** or plan. You may need to make a drawing, table, or list. You may need to use a formula. You may need to guess and then check your guess!

Whenever possible, once you know your plan, find an approximate answer. An **estimate** gives you an idea of what the answer will be *before you solve the problem.* It will help you to decide whether or not your answer, when you get it, makes sense.

Think About It

Why is it a good idea to estimate an answer before computing it?

The estimated answer will help you to decide whether or not your answer

makes sense.

Read each Example. Notice the label for the plan, such as "Add." The label is followed by a description.

Example A Mona and Joseph paddled a canoe upriver for 48 minutes. They stopped for 30 minutes to eat lunch. Then they paddled 23 minutes back downriver. How many minutes were they gone on the canoe trip?

The Plan: *Add (minutes upriver + minutes for lunch + minutes downriver = total minutes)*

The Estimate: *50 + 30 + 20 = 100*

Example B Mona and Joseph collected 18 different kinds of leaves. Mona found 4 more kinds than Joseph. How many kinds of leaves did each person find?

The Plan: *Guess and Check (Guess the number of leaves Joseph found. Add 4 for the leaves Mona found. Do the numbers total 18? If not, try another number for Joseph's leaves.)*

In Example A, the plan is to add. Notice the estimate that is made as part of this plan. In Example B, you can guess, check your guess, and then revise your guess if necessary. When you use a ''guess and check'' strategy, you cannot make an estimate.

Teacher Note: Planning what to do, Step 3 in problem solving, is the most difficult of the steps. Students may need help with these Practice items, especially item 4. Although students are not asked actually to solve these problems, the answers are provided for your information. Accept reasonable estimates.

Practice

Write a plan for solving each problem below. Label the plan and then describe it in parentheses, as was done in the Examples. Then show how you would compute an estimate based on your plan.

1. It costs $3.25 per hour to rent a canoe. How much will it cost to rent a canoe for 5 hours?

    The Plan: Multiply (cost per hour × number of hours = total cost)

    The Estimate: 3 × 5 = 15   (Computed answer: $16.25)

2. There are 27 people who want to use canoes. Each canoe holds 3 people. How many canoes are needed?

    The Plan: Divide (people who want canoes ÷ people per canoe

    = number of canoes needed)

    The Estimate: 30 ÷ 3 = 10   (Computed answer: 9 canoes)

3. Last week $123.50 was collected for canoe rentals. This week $172.25 was collected. How much more was collected this week?

    The Plan: Subtract (money collected this week − money

    collected last week = how much more money collected this week)

    The Estimate: 170 − 120 = 50   (Computed answer: $48.75)

4. Terry and Amanda took turns paddling a canoe. They paddled for a total of 45 minutes. Amanda paddled for 9 more minutes than Terry. How many minutes did each person paddle?

    The Plan: Guess and Check (Guess the number of minutes Terry

    paddled. Add 9 to find the number of minutes Amanda paddled.

    Is the total 45?)

    The Estimate: cannot be made
    (Computed answer: Terry = 18 minutes, Amanda = 27 minutes)

Additional word problems for Lesson 4 skills practice are on page 86.

Cumulative Practice: Steps 1, 2, and 3

Aim: To practice with Steps 1, 2, and 3 in combination

What You Need to Know

You have looked at Steps 1, 2, and 3 of the five-step plan for solving word problems. In Step 1, you read the problem, reread for details, and then reword the question. In Step 2, you find the needed facts. In Step 3, you plan how to use the information to answer the question. If you can, you also estimate the answer in Step 3.

Often, more than one plan can be used to solve a problem. Be sure that your plan will answer the question. Remember to visualize the problem. This will help you to choose a strategy.

Think About It

Name the first three steps in solving a word problem.

Step 1: Read the problem, reread for details, and reword the question.

Step 2: Find the needed facts.

Step 3: Plan what to do and estimate the answer.

Read each word problem below. The question is underlined. The needed data are circled. The plan and the estimate are written out.

Example A   Mike has 2 part-time jobs. He earns $2.50 per hour for babysitting and $2.25 per hour for lawn work. If he spends 3 hours mowing and raking Ms. Moy's lawn, how much will she owe him?

The Plan: *Multiply (number of hours × rate per hour = amount earned)*

The Estimate: *3 × 2 = 6*

Example B   How far is it from Leftville through Centerville to Rightville?

The Plan: *Add (miles from Leftville to Centerville + miles from Centerville to Rightville = total miles)*

The Estimate: *30 + 40 = 70*

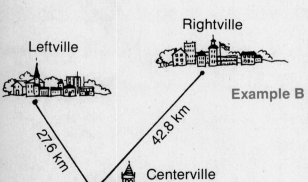

Rightville

Leftville

27.6 km   42.8 km

Centerville

Notice that there is extra (unimportant) information given in Example A. In Example B, all the needed data are shown on the diagram. The plan for solving each example is to use one of the four mathematical operations. In Example A, the plan is to multiply; in Example B, the plan is to add.

Practice

For each word problem below, underline the question. Circle the needed facts. Then write your plan and your estimate.

Bookstore Sale!
Any magazine $ .75
Any calendar $1.25
Any paperback
  book $2.65

1. How much more does a book cost than a calendar?

   The Plan: Subtract (price of book − price of calendar =

   difference in price)

   The Estimate: 2.50 − 1.00 = 1.50   ($1.40)

2. There are 210 students going on a class field trip to the state capital. Each school bus holds 42 students. How many buses are needed for the trip?

   The Plan: Divide (number of students ÷ number of students per bus

       = number of buses needed)

   The Estimate: 200 ÷ 40 = 5   (5 buses)

3. There were 24,600 fans at the ballpark on Saturday. On Sunday, there were 27,000 fans at the ballpark. How many more people were at the ballpark on Sunday than on Saturday?

   The Plan: Subtract (fans on Sunday − fans on Saturday = how many

   more people on Sunday)

   The Estimate: 27,000 − 25,000 = 2,000   (2,400 more people)

4. Maxine is taking a bus trip to visit her sister. The first leg of her trip takes $1\frac{3}{4}$ hours. She then has a $\frac{1}{4}$-hour wait before traveling for another $2\frac{1}{4}$ hours. How many hours will the total trip take?

   The Plan: Add (time for first leg + waiting time + time for second

   leg = time for total trip)

   The Estimate: 2 + 0 + 2 = 4   ($4\frac{1}{4}$ hours)

Additional word problems for Lesson 5 skills practice are on page 87.   **11**

Step Four: Carry Out the Plan

Aim: To carry out the plan for solving a word problem

What You Need to Know

After you have a plan for solving a word problem, you are ready to CARRY OUT THE PLAN. In this fourth step, you will often need to compute — to add, subtract, multiply, or divide. You may be working with whole numbers (0, 1, 2, ...), decimals (0.1, 0.2, 0.3, ...), or fractions ($\frac{1}{4}$, $\frac{1}{2}$, $\frac{3}{4}$, ...). The thing to remember is to follow your plan *step by step.* That's what it means to carry out, or execute, the plan.

You also need to think about the best "how" for executing your plan. Some problems can be solved mentally, in your head. Other problems require the use of paper and pencil. Still others are best done with a calculator. Choose the way that works best for each problem.

Think About It

What does it mean to *execute* your plan?

It means to follow or carry out the plan step by step.

Read the following word problems. Notice how the labeled plan is carried out in each example.

Example A The Pineview School yearbook sells for $4. The staff sold 515 books. How much money was collected?

The Plan: *Multiply*   **The Estimate:** *500 × 4 = 2,000*

The Execution: 515 **Computed Answer:** *$2,060*
(Use paper   × 4
and pencil.)   2,060

Example B The printer charges $300 to print 100 books. Find the cost of printing each book.

The Plan: *Divide*   **The Estimate:** *300 ÷ 100 = 3*

The Execution: 3   **Computed Answer:** *$3.00*
(Solve   100$\overline{)300}$
mentally.)

In Example A, the problem is solved using paper and pencil. The problem in Example B can be solved mentally. In both, it is a good idea to estimate the answers before computing them.

Practice

For each problem, box the plan you would use to solve it. Then estimate the answer and carry out the plan. Show your computation in the space to the right of each item. Use the information in the table if you need it.

Pineview Student Enrollment	
sixth-graders	224
seventh-graders	247
eighth-graders	319

1. How many students attend Pineview School?

The Plan: [Add] Subtract Multiply Divide Guess/Check

The Estimate: 200 + 250 + 300 = 750

Computed Answer: 790 students

1. The Execution

```
  224
  247
+ 319
  790
```

2. If 275 eighth-graders bought yearbooks, how many eighth-graders did not buy yearbooks?

The Plan: Add [Subtract] Multiply Divide Guess/Check

The Estimate: 300 − 275 = 25

Computed Answer: 44 eighth-graders

2. The Execution

```
  319
− 275
   44
```

3. Each page in the yearbook has 16 pictures. How many pages will be used for pictures of the sixth-graders?

The Plan: Add Subtract Multiply [Divide] Guess/Check

The Estimate: 200 ÷ 15 = 13

Computed Answer: 14 pages

3. The Execution

```
     14
16) 224
```

4. The yearbook committee plans to buy 26 rolls of film. Each roll costs $4.59. How much will the committee spend on film?

The Plan: Add Subtract [Multiply] Divide Guess/Check

The Estimate: 25 × 5 = 125

Computed Answer: $119.34

4. The Execution

```
   4.59
×   26
 119.34
```

Additional word problems for Lesson 6 skills practice are on page 88.

Lesson 7

Cumulative Practice: Steps 1, 2, 3, and 4

Aim: To practice with Steps 1, 2, 3, and 4 in combination

What You Need to Know

So far, you have learned four of the five steps for solving word problems. You have gone all the way from reading and rewording to carrying out a plan.

As you become more familiar with the whole five-step approach, you may find that you can do some of the steps mentally. That's great, but *never skip a step.* Each step is important for finding the correct solution.

Teacher Note: In discussion of the Example and Practice items, you may want to have students reword each underlined question.

Think About It

What might happen if you were to skip — Accept reasonable answers.

Step 1? You might misunderstand the question.

Step 2? You might miss a needed fact or use an unnecessary fact.

Step 3? You might end up using a worthless plan.

Step 4? You would get no answer.

Read the Example below. Notice how each step is completed. Step 1: The question is underlined. Step 2: The needed facts are circled. Step 3: The plan is boxed and the estimate is shown. Step 4: The execution and answer are shown.

Example   Nancy scored (15 points) during the first half of the basketball game. She scored (18 points) during the second half. Robyn scored 12 points during the first half and no points during the second half. <u>How many points did Nancy score during the whole game?</u>

The Plan: [Add]   Subtract   Multiply   Divide   Guess/Check

The Estimate: *15 + 20 = 35*

The Execution:
$$\begin{array}{r} 15 \\ +18 \\ \hline 33 \end{array}$$

Computed Answer: *33 points*

14

Did you notice the "extra" information in the Example? What piece of data is not circled?

Teacher Note: In discussion, have students tell how closely their estimates matched their computed answers.

Practice

Complete each of the four steps for these word problems. Show each step as it was shown in the Example.

1. There were (265 fans) at the game. Of these, (116 people) sat on the visitor's side. The rest sat on the home-team's side. <u>How many people sat on the home-team's side?</u>

   The Plan: Add   [Subtract]   Multiply   Divide   Guess/Check

   The Estimate: 250 − 100 = 150

   Computed Answer: 149 people

   1. The Execution

   ```
     265
   − 116
   ─────
     149
   ```

Basketball Tickets
Adults	$1.75
Students	$1.25
Children (under 10)	$1.00

2. <u>How much will the Jeffers family pay for 4 adult tickets?</u>

   The Plan: Add   Subtract   [Multiply]   Divide   Guess/Check

   The Estimate: 2.00 × 4 = 8.00

   Computed Answer: $7.00

   2. The Execution

   ```
     1.75
   ×    4
   ─────
    7.00
   ```

3. George scored (96 points) in the first (6 games) of the season. He scored the same number of points in each game. <u>How many points did George score in each game?</u>

   The Plan: Add   Subtract   Multiply   [Divide]   Guess/Check

   The Estimate: 100 ÷ 5 = 20

   Computed Answer: 16 points

   3. The Execution

   ```
      16
   6) 96
   ```

4. At the end of the first half, the Dunkers and the Swishers had scored a total of (51 points). The (Dunkers had scored 3 more points than the Swishers). <u>How many points did each team score in the first half?</u>

   The Plan: Add   Subtract   Multiply   Divide   [Guess/Check]

   The Estimate: <u>cannot be made</u>

   Computed Answer: Dunkers: 27 points; Swishers: 24 points

   4. The Execution

   Student's execution for item 4 should be a series of guessed pairs of numbers.

Additional word problems for Lesson 7 skills practice are on page 89.

Step Five: Check the Answer

Aim: To check the answer to a word problem

What You Need to Know

Teacher Note: Be sure that students understand how computation accuracy is checked by doing the computation backward. For instance, numbers can be added or multiplied in a different order. Division can be checked by multiplying the quotient by the divisor (e.g., $10 \div 2 = 5$; $5 \times 2 = 10$).

After you find an answer to a word problem, you have only one step left. You need to CHECK THE ANSWER. This is the last, and one of the most important, steps in the problem solving process.

To check your answer, do two things. First ask yourself, "Does my answer make sense? (Does it answer the question?) Is it close to my estimate?" In other words, is your answer **reasonable?** Second, if it is, check for **computation accuracy.**

Think About It

The fifth step in solving word problems has two parts. Name the two parts.

Step 5: First check that the answer is reasonable.

Then check for computation accuracy.

Read the following word problems. Notice how the two-part check is used to decide if the answer is correct.

Example A It costs $1.25 per person to enter the Wild-Eye Amusement Park. On Saturday, 153 people entered the park. How much money was collected at the gate?

The Plan: *Multiply*   **The Estimate:** *1.0 × 150 = 150*

The Execution: *1.25*   **Computed Answer:** *$181.25*
$$\begin{array}{r} 1.25 \\ \times 153 \\ \hline 181.25 \end{array}$$

The Check: *Is answer reasonable? Yes.* (It is reasonably close to the estimated answer.)
Does computation check? No. (Dividing 181.25 by 1.25 gives 145, not 153.)

Example B There were 33 people who took the Spaceship ride in the morning. There were 53 people who took it in the afternoon. How many people rode the Spaceship in all?

The Plan: *Add*   **The Estimate:** *30 + 50 = 80*

The Execution: *33*   **Computed Answer:** *20 people*
$$\begin{array}{r} 33 \\ + 53 \\ \hline 20 \end{array}$$

The Check: *Is answer reasonable? No.* (How can fewer people ride in all than rode on either trip?)

In Example A, the answer is reasonable, but the computation does not check. In Example B, the answer is not reasonable. It does not make sense (and it is not close to the estimate).

Teacher Note: Students may need help with Practice item 3. The computation checks as accurate and is close to the estimate, *given the plan to multiply*. Yet the answer is not reasonable, since it means that Michael went on more rides each visit than he did altogether in 3 visits. Be sure students understand that this situation indicates an incorrect plan (Step 3).

Practice

For each problem, study how Steps 3 and 4 were done. Then use the two-part check to decide if the computed answer is a correct answer. If it is not, correct it.

1. Hot-air balloon rides are given 4 times each day. Tickets for a balloon ride are $5.25 for adults and $2.75 for children. On one trip, 8 adults and no children rode in the balloon. How much money was collected for this trip?

   The Plan: Multiply

   The Execution: 5.25
   $\underline{\times 8}$
   42.80

   The Estimate: $8 \times 5 = 40$

   Computed Answer: $42.80

   The Check: The answer is reasonable. The computation is wrong.

   $(42.80 \div 8 = 5.35)$ Correct answer: $42.00

parking lot

 Fun House

$1\frac{1}{2}$ miles

$\frac{3}{4}$ mile

2 miles

Pirate's Cove

2. Susan and Terry are planning to walk from the parking lot to the Fun House and then to Pirate's Cove before returning to the parking lot. How many miles will they walk in all?

   The Plan: Add

   The Execution:
   $\frac{6}{4} + \frac{8}{4} + \frac{3}{4} = 4\frac{1}{4}$

   The Estimate: $1\frac{1}{2} + 2 + 1 = 4\frac{1}{2}$

   Computed Answer: $4\frac{1}{4}$ miles

   The Check: The answer is reasonable. The computation is correct.

   $(^3/_4 + ^8/_4 + ^6/_4 = 4^1/_4)$

3. Michael went on 42 different rides during his 3 visits to the park. He went on the same number of rides each visit. How many different rides did he go on each visit?

   The Plan: Multiply

   The Execution: 42
   $\underline{\times 3}$
   126

   The Estimate: $40 \times 3 = 120$

   Computed Answer: 126 different rides

   The Check: The answer is not reasonable. The computation checks.

   Choose new plan. Divide: $42 \div 3 = 14$. Correct answer: 14 different rides

Additional word problems for Lesson 8 skills practice are on page 90.   **17**

Cumulative Practice: Steps 1, 2, 3, 4, and 5

Aim: To practice with Steps 1, 2, 3, 4, and 5 in combination

What You Need to Know

There is no magic formula or single set of rules you can use to solve all word problems. The five steps you have learned are a *guide* to problem solving. They lead the way.

Along the way, there are times you will choose a plan that does not give a reasonable or accurate solution. When that happens, relax! Reread the problem and try another plan.

Don't try to take short-cuts by skipping steps or by going too fast. Take each step in order, thinking as you go.

Teacher Note: Discuss the art at the top of page 19. Point out how the symbol reflects the five steps in problem solving. Tell students that this symbol will appear in each lesson in the rest of the book, reminding

Think About It them never to skip a step.

Suppose you follow all five steps and still do not get the correct answer. What three things should you do?

Relax, reread the problem, and try another plan.

Read the word problem below. Notice how all five steps are used to solve the problem.

Example In a swimming relay, Lara swam the first lap in 31.6 seconds. Louise swam the second lap in 30.5 seconds. Linda swam the third lap in 29.1 seconds. How long did it take the girls to swim the 3 laps altogether?

The Question Reworded: *What was the girls' total swimming time?* (Question is underlined above.)

The Facts: *Lara: 31.6 sec.; Louise: 30.5 sec.; Linda: 29.1 sec.* (Needed facts are circled.)

The Plan: *Add* **The Estimate:** *30 + 30 + 30 = 90*

Execution:
```
  31.6
  30.5
 +29.1
  91.2
```
Computed Answer: *91.2 seconds*

The Check: *Answer is reasonable.* (It is close to the estimate and it makes sense.)

Computation is correct. (Adding backward gives the same answer.)

The Example serves as a review of the five-step process for solving word problems. Be sure you have thought through the Example carefully before doing the Practice items below.

Practice

For each problem below, underline the question and circle the needed facts. Then write the plan and estimate the answer. Finally, carry out the plan and check the answer.

1. Bonita's Boutique is having a summer sale. A coat that usually sells for $79.95 can be bought on sale for $67.99. How much can be saved by buying the coat during the sale?

   The Plan: _Subtract_   The Estimate: _80 − 70 = 10_

   Computed Answer: _$11.96_   The Check: _The answer is_
   reasonable. The computation is correct.

   1. The Execution

   79.95
   − 67.99
   11.96

2. Joel, Aaron, Jason, and Melissa gave a Halloween party. They spent $31.92 on refreshments and decorations. If they shared the cost equally, how much did each person pay?

   The Plan: _Divide_   The Estimate: _32 ÷ 4 = 8_

   Computed Answer: _$7.98_   The Check: _The answer is_
   reasonable. The computation is correct.

   2. The Execution

   7.98
   4) 31.92

3. The base price of a new car is $6,580. A radio costs $225, and air conditioning costs $575. What is the price of a new car with these two extras?

   The Plan: _Add_   The Estimate: _6,500 + 200 +_
                                            _600 = 7,300_
   Computed Answer: _$7,380_   The Check: _The answer is_
   reasonable. The computation is correct.

   3. The Execution

   6,580
   225
   + 575
   7,380

4. Juan's mother purchased 4 new tires for her car. The total bill came to $255.92. What was the cost per tire?

   The Plan: _Divide_   The Estimate: _240 ÷ 4 = 60_

   Computed Answer: _$63.98_   The Check: _The answer is_
   reasonable. The computation is correct.

   4. The Execution

   63.98
   4) 255.92

Additional word problems for Lesson 9 skills practice are on page 91.

Unit 1 Review

A. On each line, write **T** or **F** to tell whether the statement is true or false.

_T_

1. The first step in solving any word problem is to read the problem all the way through, reread the problem more slowly, and reword the question.

_F_

2. Being able to reword the question shows that you have found the important data in the problem.

_F_

3. The facts needed to solve a word problem are always found "inside" the problem.

_T_

4. When you *visualize* a word problem, you form a picture in your mind of what is going on in the problem.

_F_

5. All word problems can be solved by either adding, subtracting, multiplying, or dividing.

_T_

6. Often, more than one plan can be used to solve a word problem.

_T_

7. When you *execute* a plan for solving a word problem, you carry out the plan step-by-step.

_F_

8. As you become familiar with the five-step approach to solving problems, it is sometimes a good idea to skip the "easy" steps.

_T_

9. When you check an answer, you should check for reasonableness and for computation accuracy.

_F_

10. If you follow the five-step approach to solving problems, you will always get a correct answer on your first try.

B. On each line, write the word that best completes the sentence.

question

11. A word problem can be divided into two basic parts—the information and the ____.

facts (or data)

12. In Step 2 of the problem-solving process, you must find the ____ you need to solve the problem.

estimate

13. The ____ gives you an idea of what the answer to a word problem will be *before* you solve the problem.

carry out (or execute)

14. After you have a plan for solving a word problem, you are ready to ____ the plan.

check

15. The last step in solving any word problem is to ____ the answer.

C. Circle the letter of the correct answer.

Sue and Al are in training for the school track team. On Monday, Sue jogged for 28 minutes and did 25 leg lifts. Al jogged for 19 minutes and did 35 leg lifts. How much longer did Sue jog than Al?

16. Which question is a rewording of the question in the word problem above?
    a. Who jogged longer?
    b. How many more leg lifts did Al do than Sue?
    c. How many more minutes did Sue jog than Al?
    d. How long would Sue jog in two days?

17. Which of these is a needed fact for solving the problem above?
    a. Sue and Al are in training.   c. Al did 35 leg lifts.
    b. Sue jogged for 28 minutes.   d. Sue and Al jogged on Monday.

18. Which of these is a plan for solving the word problem above?
    a. Add (minutes Sue jogged + minutes Al jogged)
    b. Subtract (minutes Al jogged – minutes Sue jogged)
    c. Add (leg lifts Sue did + left lifts Al did)
    d. Subtract (minutes Sue jogged – minutes Al jogged)

19. Which of these shows a way to estimate the answer to the problem above?
    a. 30 – 20 = 10   b. 20 – 10 = 10   c. 30 + 20 = 50   d. 20 + 10 = 30

20. Raul bought 2 new tires for his bike. The total bill was $36.50. How much did he pay for each tire?
    a. $73.00   b. $18.25   c. $182.50   d. $730.00

21. There are 30 students in a computer class. Each student wrote 3 programs. How many programs were written in all?
    a. 10 programs   b. 27 programs   c. 90 programs   d. 33 programs

22. Fran walked $2\frac{1}{2}$ miles to the book store and then $1\frac{1}{2}$ miles to Beth's house. How far did she walk in all?
    a. 3 miles   b. 4 miles   c. $3\frac{1}{2}$ miles   d. $4\frac{1}{2}$ miles

23. Rosa delivered 185 newspapers on Saturday and 297 newspapers on Sunday. How many papers did she deliver in all?
    a. 472 papers   b. 112 papers   c. 382 papers   d. 482 papers

24. Which of these is NOT a reasonable answer to the problem in item 23?
    a. 282 papers   b. 482 papers   c. 472 papers   d. 492 papers

25. Which of these shows a way to check the computation for the problem in item 23?
    a.   297   b.   297   c.   297   d. 185)297
        + 185   – 185   × 185

Go on to the next page.

D. Read and reread each word problem. Then follow the directions to show your solution to the problem.

26. Tickets to the Cinema Movie Theater are $4.25 for adults and $2.25 for children. How much did the Golds spend for 3 adult tickets?

   a. Underline the question.
   b. Circle the needed facts in the problem.

   c. Describe your plan: _Multiply (price of adult ticket × number of adult_

   tickets = total price)

   d. If an estimate can be made, show it here: _4 × 3 = 12_

   e. Carry out your plan. Answer: _$12.75_   (4.25 × 3 = 12.75)

   f. Check your answer. If you got an incorrect answer, tell how you know it is wrong. Then write the correct answer.

   Students who got incorrect answers should mention computation error or

   that the answer was not reasonable.

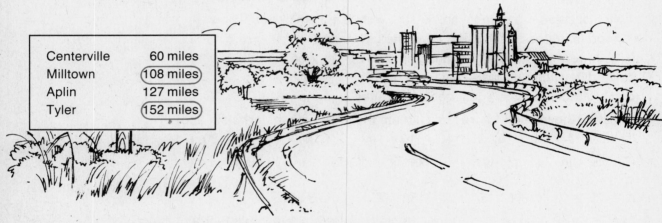

Centerville	60 miles
Milltown	108 miles
Aplin	127 miles
Tyler	152 miles

27. From the sign, how much farther is it to Tyler than to Milltown?

   a. Underline the question.
   b. Circle the needed facts in the problem.

   c. Describe your plan: _Subtract (miles to Tyler – miles to Milltown = miles_

   farther to Tyler than to Milltown)

   d. If an estimate can be made, show it here: _150 – 110 = 40_

   e. Carry out your plan. Answer: _44 miles_   (152 – 108 = 44)

   f. Check your answer. If you got an incorrect answer, tell how you know it is wrong. Then write the correct answer.

   Students who got incorrect answers should mention computation error or

   that the answer was not reasonable.

2 Developing Your Problem Solving Skills

■ Too Much Information ■ Too Little Information ■ Reading a Diagram ■ Reading a Table ■ Reading a Graph ■ Using the Appendix ■ Add or Subtract? ■ Multiply or Divide? ■ Interpret the Remainder ■ Cumulative Practice: Choosing the Operation ■ Two-Operation Problems ■ Choosing a Sensible Answer ■ Checking Estimates and Computations

Too Much Information

Aim: To identify the needed facts in a problem that also contains unneeded information

What You Need to Know

Your own problems are rarely as neat and tidy as those you read about in textbooks. In real life, there are often a lot of facts available to you. Many of these facts are not needed to solve the problem. In order to solve real-life problems, first you identify the question. Then you separate the useful facts from the ones you do not need.

Ask yourself, "Which of these facts do I need to find the answer to the question?" Always keep in mind the question you are trying to answer.

Think About It

Name one way in which real-life problems often differ from many textbook problems.

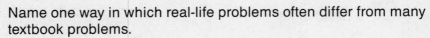
Real-life problems often include a lot of facts that are not needed to

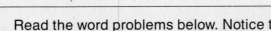
solve the problems.

Read the word problems below. Notice the needed facts. In each problem, there are circles around the important facts. The unnecessary facts are crossed out.

Example A There are ⟨12 teams⟩ in the South County Soccer League. There are ⟨14 players⟩ and 2 ̶c̶o̶a̶c̶h̶e̶s̶ on each team. How many players are in the South County Soccer League?

The Execution: 14
                    × 12
                    ———
                    168

Answer: *168 players*

Example B In the first half of a game, the Goalbusters scored ⟨3 goals⟩ and the Falcons scored ⟨4 goals⟩. During the second half, the Goalbusters and the Falcons each scored ⟨2 goals⟩. Each half of the game was 2̶5̶ ̶m̶i̶n̶u̶t̶e̶s̶. There was a 1̶0̶-̶m̶i̶n̶u̶t̶e̶ intermission between halves. What was the final score of the game?

The Execution: 3   4
                    +2   +2
                    ——   ——
                     5   6

Answer: *Goalbusters 5, Falcons 6*

In Example A, there is one piece of unnecessary data. To answer the question about the number of players, you don't need to know the number of coaches. So, the unnecessary fact that there are "2 coaches" is crossed out. In Example B, the facts that relate to the time are not important. They are crossed out.

Teacher Note: Remind students that they need to perform all five steps in the Practice problems, even though they are only showing Step 2 (finding the needed facts) and Step 3 (stating the plan) plus the answer. Remind students also to estimate as part of their plan. Check that students' answers include correct unit labels.

Practice

For each problem below, reword the question to yourself. Circle the needed facts. Cross out the unnecessary facts. Write the plan. Carry out the plan mentally, with paper and pencil, or with a calculator. Write the answer.

Peanuts	35¢
Popcorn	40¢
Milk	
large	45¢
small	30¢

1. Judy and Juan worked at the refreshment stand from 9:00 A.M. to 1:00 P.M. During this time, they sold 26 boxes of popcorn. How much money did they take in on the sale of the popcorn?

   The Plan: _Multiply_   Answer: _$10.40_
   _____ $(26 \times .40 = 10.40)$

2. At 1:00 P.M. Teena and Terrance started working at the stand. They worked for $3\frac{1}{2}$ hours and then closed the stand. During this time, they sold 47 large milks and 53 small milks. What time was the refreshment stand closed?

   The Plan: _Add_   Answer: _4:30 P.M._
   (1 hr. 0 min. + 3 hr. 30 min. = 4 hr. 30 min.)

3. During the 12-game season, the Falcons scored a total of 42 goals in official games and 53 goals in practice games. What was the average number of points they scored in official games? (Hint: To find an average, you divide a total by the number of groups involved.)

   The Plan: _Divide_   Answer: _3.5 points_
   _____ $(42 \div 12 = 3.5)$

4. At the first game of the season, 127 fans sat in the bleachers and 65 fans sat in lawn chairs. At the second game, 89 fans sat in the bleachers and 21 fans sat in lawn chairs. How many more people sat in the bleachers during the first game than the second game?

   The Plan: _Subtract_   Answer: _38 more fans_
   _____ $(127 - 89 = 38)$

5. During the 12-game season, the Goalbusters won $\frac{1}{2}$ of their games, lost $\frac{1}{3}$ of their games, and tied $\frac{1}{6}$ of their games. How many games did they tie during the season?

   The Plan: _Multiply_   Answer: _2 games_
   _____ $(\frac{1}{6} \times 12 = 2)$

Additional word problems for Lesson 10 skills practice are on page 92.

Too Little Information

> **Aim:** To recognize when there is not enough information to solve a problem

What You Need to Know

In the last lesson, you looked at problems that had too many facts. Here you will see problems that have too few facts. These problems cannot be solved with the facts given.

First be sure you understand the question. Next think, "What facts do I need to know to solve this problem?" Remember to look for data both "inside" and "outside" the problem. Unless you can find all the needed facts, you cannot solve the problem.

Teacher Note: Go over each example carefully with students. Be sure they understand why the problem cannot be solved without the missing fact. Have students explain why the unhelpful facts (the ones that are not underlined) are indeed unhelpful.

Think About It

What do you need to solve any problem?

You must have all the important facts, or needed data.

Read the problems below. Each is missing an important fact.

Example A Sarah, Jessie, and Carmen scored a total of 24 goals during the soccer season. How many goals did each girl score?

Missing Fact: *how the three girls scored in relation to each other*

- *Jessie scored as well as Sarah.*
- *Two girls scored more than 6 goals each.*
- *The girls each scored the same number of goals.*

The Execution: $\dfrac{8}{3) \overline{24}}$ **Answer:** *8 goals*

Example B Keith dribbled the ball for $7\frac{1}{2}$ yards before passing it to Scott. Scott continued to dribble until he kicked the ball into the goal from the 10-yard line. How far did Scott and Keith dribble the ball in all?

Missing Fact: *how far Scott dribbled the ball*

- *Keith started dribbling at the 20-yard line.*
- *Scott dribbled the ball for $11\frac{1}{2}$ yards.*
- *Scott dribbled farther than Keith.*

The Execution:
$$\begin{array}{r} 7\frac{1}{2} \\ +11\frac{1}{2} \\ \hline 19 \end{array}$$
Answer: *19 yards*

In Example A, you need to know that each girl scored the same number of goals. In Example B, there is both unneeded information (10-yard line) and missing information.

Practice

Describe each missing fact as done in the Examples. <u>Underline</u> the fact that meets the need. Write the plan and the answer.

1. Ling bought a new soccer ball. He gave the clerk in the shop a $20 bill. How much change did Ling receive?

   Missing Fact: <u>how much the soccer ball cost</u>

   - <u>The ball cost $14.95.</u>
   - There were 5 different types of soccer balls at the shop.
   - Soccer balls cost more than footballs.

   The Plan: <u>Subtract</u>   Answer: $5.05
                                    (20.00 − 14.95 = 5.05)

2. The coach ordered a trophy for each of the 16 players on his team. The trophies will be ready in 2 weeks. How much will all the trophies cost?

   Missing Fact: <u>how much each trophy costs</u>

   - The trophies were ordered on October 2.
   - Trophies cost more than prize ribbons.
   - <u>The trophies cost $5.25 each.</u>

   The Plan: <u>Multiply</u>   Answer: $84.00
                                    (5.25 × 16 = 84)

3. New soccer balls were given out evenly among the 12 teams. How many new soccer balls did each team get?

   Missing Fact: <u>how many new balls were given out altogether</u>

   - Each team now has 7 old soccer balls.
   - Last year each team received 4 new soccer balls.
   - <u>There were 72 new soccer balls given out.</u>

   The Plan: <u>Divide</u>   Answer: 6 soccer balls
                                    (72 ÷ 12 = 6)

4. Since the start of the season, the soccer team has practiced $1\frac{1}{2}$ hours on Mondays and 1 hour on Wednesdays. How many hours have they practiced in all?

   Missing Fact: <u>how many weeks have gone by</u>

   - <u>The soccer season began 5 weeks ago.</u>
   - They are not yet halfway through the soccer season.
   - The tennis team practices for 3 hours each week.

   The Plan: <u>Multiply</u>   Answer: $12\frac{1}{2}$ hours
                                    $(5 \times 2\frac{1}{2} = 12\frac{1}{2})$

Reading a Diagram

Aim: To locate needed facts on a simple line diagram

What You Need to Know

Sometimes, facts may be found in diagrams and drawings. You know that you have to read all the words in a problem before you can pick the key words. You must also "read" a whole diagram before you can pick the needed facts from it.

When you have a problem with a diagram, do these three things:

- First, read the problem and understand the question.
- Second, study the diagram.
- Third, reread the problem while you locate the needed facts in the diagram.

Think About It

Suppose you tried finding needed facts in a diagram before you had studied the whole diagram. What might happen?

You might miss an important fact or pick an unimportant fact.

Read the word problems below. Notice where the facts needed to solve the problems are located.

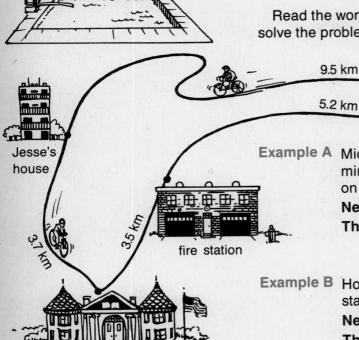

swimming pool

9.5 km

Michael's house

5.2 km

Jesse's house

3.7 km

3.5 km

fire station

library

Example A Michael rode his bike from his house past the swimming pool to Jesse's house and then back to his house on the same street. How far did he ride?

Needed Diagram Facts: *9.5 km*

The Execution:
$$\begin{array}{r} 9.5 \\ \times\,2 \\ \hline 19.0 \end{array}$$

Answer: *19 km*

Example B How much farther is it from Michael's house to the fire station than it is from the fire station to the library?

Needed Diagram Facts: *5.2 km; 3.5 km*

The Execution:
$$\begin{array}{r} 5.2 \\ -\,3.5 \\ \hline 1.7 \end{array}$$

Answer: *1.7 km*

In both Examples A and B, the facts needed to solve the problems are in the diagram. In Example A, there is also a piece of data "inside" the word problem. It tells you that Michael rode to and from Jesse's house, past the swimming pool, on the same street. That is how you know to use the number 2 during the execution of the plan.

Practice

For each problem, write the facts you will use from the diagram. Write the plan and the answer. (Don't skip any of the five steps, though!) For items 1 and 2, use the diagram on page 28.

1. Jesse rode his bike from his home, past the library and the fire station, to Michael's house. How far did he ride?

   Needed Diagram Facts: <u>3.7 km; 3.5 km; 5.2 km</u>

   The Plan: <u>Add</u>   Answer: <u>12.4 km</u>
   $$(3.7 + 3.5 + 5.2 = 12.4)$$

2. Michael always takes the shortest route from his house to Jesse's house. In 1 week he made 3 round trips to Jesse's house on his bike. How far did he ride his bike that week?

   Needed Diagram Facts: <u>9.5 km</u>

   The Plan: <u>Multiply</u>   Answer: <u>57 km</u>
   $$(3 \times 2 \times 9.5 = 57)$$

3. Julie is on the basketball team at school. The diagram shows the path she follows when she jogs before school each morning. How many miles does Julie jog each morning?

   Needed Diagram Facts: <u>½ mi.; 1¼ mi.; ¾ mi.; 1½ mi.; ½ mi.</u>

   The Plan: <u>Add</u>   Answer: <u>4½ miles</u>
   $$(\tfrac{2}{4} + \tfrac{5}{4} + \tfrac{3}{4} + \tfrac{6}{4} + \tfrac{2}{4} = \tfrac{18}{4} = 4\tfrac{1}{2})$$

4. Julie follows this same path 5 mornings each week. How far does she jog each week?

   Needed Diagram Facts: <u>same as item 3 (using answer to item 3)</u>

   The Plan: <u>Multiply</u>   Answer: <u>22½ miles</u>
   $$(5 \times 4\tfrac{1}{2} = 22\tfrac{1}{2})$$

5. One morning, Julie followed her usual path until she got to Debbie's house. Then she turned around and took the same path home. How far did she jog that morning?

   Needed Diagram Facts: <u>½ mi.; 1¼ mi.</u>

   The Plan: <u>Add and multiply</u>   Answer: <u>3½ miles</u>
   $$(\tfrac{2}{4} + \tfrac{5}{4} = \tfrac{7}{4}; \tfrac{7}{4} \times 2 = \tfrac{14}{4} = 3\tfrac{1}{2})$$

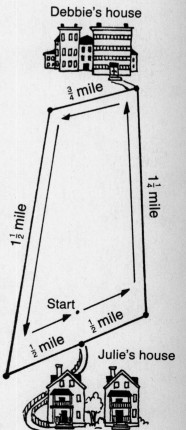

Debbie's house

¾ mile

1¼ mile

1½ mile

Start

½ mile

½ mile

Julie's house

Additional word problems for Lesson 12 skills practice are on page 94.

Lesson 13

Reading a Table

Aim: To locate needed facts in a table or chart

What You Need to Know

Facts that are "outside" a problem may appear in a table or chart. A table shows facts in a very clear way. Sometimes, when information is in a paragraph, it is hard to see how all the facts fit together. A table makes it easier to see patterns in the data.

What's the first thing you should do when you see a table? Read its title and any headings. These will give you a quick understanding of what the table is about.

Teacher Note: Have students use their hands to cover the title and headings on the table on this page. Elicit what a confusing

Think About It table it becomes without those words to explain it.

In what order are the numbers listed under the heading "1984" below?

The numbers are listed in descending or decreasing order.

Read the Example problem. Notice where the facts are found.

Busiest U.S. Airports	Take-offs and Landings	
	1984	1983
Chicago O'Hare International	741,296	671,724
Atlanta International	689,482	612,791
Van Nuys	575,721	494,273
Los Angeles International	550,758	506,076
Dallas/Ft. Worth Regional	524,564	435,533
Denver Stapleton International	512,520	458,060
Santa Ana	488,540	457,805
Long Beach	449,208	422,196
San Francisco	403,850	364,791
Phoenix Sky Harbor	399,298	346,722
St. Louis International	395,906	361,724
Boston Logan	387,422	351,474

Source: Federal Aviation Administration

Example How many more take-offs and landings were there at Atlanta International airport in 1984 than in 1983?

Needed Table Facts: *689,482; 612,791*

The Execution: *689,482*
− 612,791
76,691

Answer: *76,691 take-offs and landings*

In the Example, the facts needed to solve the problem are in the table. The problem refers to only one airport. You need to look in both columns "1984" and "1983" for the needed data.

Practice

For each problem, write the facts you will use from the table. Then write the plan and the answer. (Remember to follow all five steps.) For items 1, 2, and 3, use the table on page 30.

1. What was the total number of take-offs and landings at Long Beach during 1983 and 1984?

   Needed Table Facts: 449,208; 422,196

   The Plan: Add   Answer: 871,404 take-offs and landings
   (449,208 + 422,196 = 871,404)

2. How many more take-offs and landings were there at San Francisco in 1983 than at Phoenix Sky Harbor the same year?

   Needed Table Facts: 364,791; 346,722

   The Plan: Subtract   Answer: 18,069 take-offs and landings
   (364,791 − 346,722 = 18,069)

3. What was the average number of take-offs and landings per month at Denver Stapleton in 1984? (Remember, to find an average, divide a total by the number of groups involved.)

   Needed Table Facts: 512,520

   The Plan: Divide   Answer: 42,710 take-offs and landings
   (512,520 ÷ 12 = 42,710)

Population

City	1980	1950	1900
Chicago, IL	3,005,072	3,620,962	1,698,575
Houston, TX	1,595,138	596,163	44,633
Los Angeles, CA	2,966,850	1,970,358	102,479
New York, NY	7,071,639	7,891,957	3,437,202
Philadelphia, PA	1,688,210	2,071,605	1,293,697

Source: U.S. Bureau of the Census

4. How many fewer people lived in Philadelphia in 1980 than in 1950?

   Needed Table Facts: 2,071,605; 1,688,210

   The Plan: Subtract   Answer: 383,395 people
   (2,071,605 − 1,688,210 = 383,395)

5. In 1900, how many more people lived in the most-populated city than in the least-populated city (of the cities listed)?

   Needed Table Facts: 3,437,202 (New York); 44,633 (Houston)

   The Plan: Subtract   Answer: 3,392,569 people
   (3,437,202 − 44,633 = 3,392,569)

Additional word problems for Lesson 13 skills practice are on page 95.

Reading a Graph

Aim: To locate needed facts in a bar graph or pictograph

What You Need to Know

In this lesson, you will look at **pictographs** and **bar graphs.** Both show information in "picture" form. They make it easy to *compare* facts, to see how they relate to each other.

As when you read a table, the first thing to do with a graph is to read its title and headings. If you don't do this, you will have no idea what the "pictures" stand for.

Think About It

Read the labels (all the words) in the pictograph on this page. What does each symbol stand for?

Each symbol stands for 50 cans.

Read the word problem below. Notice where the facts are found.

**Aluminum Cans Collected
by Collins School Classes**

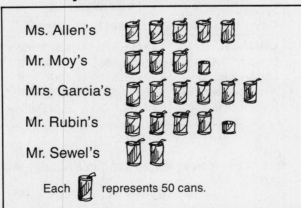

Example Five classes at Collins School are collecting cans for an anti-litter project. About how many cans have been collected by Ms. Allen's and Mr. Moy's classes together?

Needed Graph Facts: 5×50; $3\frac{1}{2} \times 50$

The Execution:

$$
\begin{array}{ccc}
50 & 50 & 250 \\
\times 5 & \times 3.5 & +175 \\
\hline
250 & 175 & 425
\end{array}
$$

Answer: *about 425 cans*

In the Example, the needed facts are in the pictograph. If you did not read all the labels, you might think that each symbol meant only one can. Then your answer would be "about 8 cans." You would think that the classes weren't trying very hard!

Practice

Write the facts you will use from the graph. Then write the plan and the answer. For items 1 and 2, use the graph on page 32.

1. About how many more cans did Mr. Rubin's class collect than Mr. Sewel's class?

   Needed Graph Facts: $4\frac{1}{2} \times 50; 2 \times 50$

   The Plan: Subtract   Answer: about 125 more cans
   (225 − 100 = 125)

2. About how many cans were collected by all five classes?

   Needed Graph Facts: $5 \times 50; 3\frac{1}{2} \times 50; 6 \times 50; 4\frac{1}{2} \times 50; 2 \times 50$

   The Plan: Add   Answer: about 1,050 cans
   (250 + 175 + 300 + 225 + 100 = 1,050)

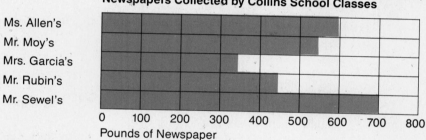

Newspapers Collected by Collins School Classes

Ms. Allen's
Mr. Moy's
Mrs. Garcia's
Mr. Rubin's
Mr. Sewel's

0 100 200 300 400 500 600 700 800
Pounds of Newspaper

3. The same classes collected newspapers. How many more pounds of paper did Mr. Sewel's class collect than Mrs. Garcia's?

   Needed Graph Facts: 700; 350

   The Plan: Subtract   Answer: about 350 more pounds
   (700 − 350 = 350)

4. Mr. Rubin's class wants to double the amount of paper they have collected by the end of the next week. If they succeed, about how many pounds of paper will they have?

   Needed Graph Facts: 450

   The Plan: Multiply   Answer: about 900 pounds
   (2 × 450 = 900)

5. There are 25 students in Ms. Allen's class. Each student collected the same amount of paper. About how many pounds of paper did each student collect?

   Needed Graph Facts: 600

   The Plan: Divide   Answer: about 24 pounds
   (600 ÷ 25 = 24)

Teacher Note: After students have completed this lesson, you may want to have them make a bar graph from the pictograph on page 32, and a pictograph from the bar graph on page 33. This activity will help students to understand the importance of titles and labels on graphs.

Additional word problems for Lesson 14 skills practice are on page 96.

Using the Appendix

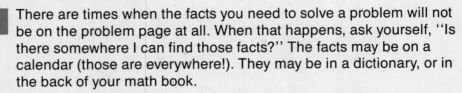

Aim: To locate needed facts in an appendix

What You Need to Know

There are times when the facts you need to solve a problem will not be on the problem page at all. When that happens, ask yourself, "Is there somewhere I can find those facts?" The facts may be on a calendar (those are everywhere!). They may be in a dictionary, or in the back of your math book.

To solve problems in this lesson, you will need information from another part of this book. Look now at the Appendix on pages 121–122.

Think About It

Name two of the sections found in the Appendix in this book.

Students should list two of the following: Table of Measures, Time,

Operations Chart, Geometric Formulas

Read the problems below. Check the Appendix in each case to see where the facts are found.

Example A Jay had 2 cups of muffin batter. He poured the batter into mini-muffin cups that held 1 ounce each. How many muffins did he make?

Needed Appendix Facts: *1 cup = 8 ounces*

The Execution: $\begin{array}{r} 2.5 \\ \times 8 \\ \hline 20 \end{array}$ **Answer:** *20 muffins*

Example B Linda has a collection of marbles weighing 4,500 grams. How many kilograms of marbles has Linda collected?

Needed Appendix Facts: *1 kilogram = 1,000 grams*

The Execution: $\begin{array}{r} 4\ r500 \\ 1{,}000\overline{)4{,}500} \end{array}$ **Answer:** *4.5 kilograms*

The facts needed to solve both Examples A and B can be found in the Appendix on pages 121–122. In Example A, you need to *convert,* or change, cups to ounces. In Example B, you need to convert grams to kilograms.

Teacher Note: Students may need help in item 4. If they have gotten ''lazy'' about following all five steps, they may only skim the question and miss the second step needed in the execution. If students show the answer as ''21 yards,'' remind them that the question asked how many yards of fence *each person* painted.

Practice

For each problem, write the facts you will use from the Appendix. Then write the plan and the answer. Remember to follow all five problem solving steps, including the check on your answer. Does each answer make sense?

1. How many feet longer is a nautical mile than a regular mile?

   Needed Appendix Facts: 1 mi. = 5,280 ft.; 1 naut. mi. = 6,076 ft.

   The Plan: Subtract   Answer: 796 feet longer
   $$(6,076 - 5,280 = 796)$$

2. The Gindoffs bought a $\frac{3}{4}$-hectare lot. How many square meters is their new lot?

   Needed Appendix Facts: 1 hectare = 10,000 square meters

   The Plan: Multiply   Answer: 7,500 square meters
   $$(\tfrac{3}{4} \times 10,000 = 7,500)$$

3. The volume of a swimming pool is 3,888 cubic feet. How many cubic yards is it?

   Needed Appendix Facts: 27 cubic feet = 1 cubic yard

   The Plan: Divide   Answer: 144 cubic yards
   $$(3,888 \div 27 = 144)$$

4. Sheryl, Max, and Beth are painting a fence that is 63 feet long. If they each paint an equal portion of the fence, how many yards of fence will they each paint?

   Needed Appendix Facts: 1 yard = 3 feet

   The Plan: Divide twice   Answer: 7 yards
   $$(63 \div 3 = 21; 21 \div 3 = 7)$$

5. If each of the 3 people uses 6 quarts of paint, how many gallons of paint will be used in all?

   Needed Appendix Facts: 4 quarts = 1 gallon

   The Plan: Multiply and divide   Answer: 4 gallons
   $$(3 \times 6 = 18; 18 \div 4 = 4\tfrac{1}{2})$$

Additional word problems for Lesson 15 skills practice are on page 97.

35

Add or Subtract?

Aim: To understand when to use addition and when to use subtraction to solve a word problem

What You Need to Know

Teacher Note: Help students understand the difference between the two actions that suggest subtraction. "Separating objects" involves a total that is broken down into parts. "Comparing two groups" involves groups that are already separate but are being compared. You may want to use Example A and Practice item 4 to demonstrate the difference.

Some problems are *routine*. They are pretty easy to solve. You only need to add, subtract, multiply, or divide. To choose the operation, *visualize* the event being described. Study the chart.

Choose Addition or Subtraction

Action	Operation
Joining different-sized groups (a different number in each group) to find a total	Addition
Separating objects to find a group that is left or **Comparing two groups** to find the difference	Subtraction

Think About It

Why is it important to visualize what is happening in a problem?

If you can visualize the events, you can choose the

operation needed to solve the problem.

Read the problems below. Visualize the action in each.

Example A On January 5, Snowball Ski Resort sold 157 ski passes. Of these, 73 were 1-day passes. The rest were weekend passes. How many weekend passes were sold?

The Action: *Separating objects*

The Operation: *Subtraction*

The Execution: 157   **Answer:** *84 weekend passes*
$$\begin{array}{r} 157 \\ -\ 73 \\ \hline 84 \end{array}$$

Example B On Saturday, $20\frac{1}{2}$ inches of snow fell on the mountain. The next day another $5\frac{3}{4}$ inches fell. How much snow fell in the two days?

The Action: *Joining different-sized groups*

The Operation: *Addition*

The Execution: $20\frac{1}{2} = \frac{41}{2} = \frac{82}{4}$; $5\frac{3}{4} = \frac{23}{4}$; $\frac{82}{4} + \frac{23}{4} = \frac{105}{4} = 26\frac{1}{4}$

Answer: $26\frac{1}{4}$ *inches*

After "The Action" heading in each example, a short version of the whole action from the chart is listed. Think about the whole action, even when you write only the first few words of it.

Teacher Note: Check that students are aware that "48 bran muffins" in item 2 is unimportant information.

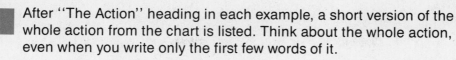

Practice

For each problem, visualize the action described. Then write the action, the operation, and the answer. (Be sure to check your answers. Do they agree with the estimates you made? Do they make sense?)

1. There are two dining rooms at the ski resort. One dining room seats 75 people. The other seats 84 people. How many people can be seated in the two dining rooms at the same time?

   The Action: <u>Joining different-sized groups</u>

   The Operation: <u>Addition</u>   Answer: <u>159 people</u>
                                             $(75 + 84 = 159)$

2. The cook filled the pot in the snack bar with 150 cups of hot chocolate and made 48 bran muffins. During the day, 79 cups of hot chocolate were served. How many cups are left in the pot?

   The Action: <u>Separating objects</u>

   The Operation: <u>Subtraction</u>   Answer: <u>71 cups</u>
                                             $(150 - 79 = 71)$

3. Amy stayed at the resort for a weekend. She spent $62.50 for her room, $47.75 on meals, and $45.00 for ski-lift tickets. How much did she spend in all?

   The Action: <u>Joining different-sized groups</u>

   The Operation: <u>Addition</u>   Answer: <u>$155.25</u>
                               $(62.50 + 47.75 + 45.00 = 155.25)$

4. There are two ski trails from the top of Mt. Snowball. The Expert trail is $1\frac{1}{2}$ miles long. The Beginner trail is $2\frac{1}{4}$ miles long. How much longer is the Beginner trail than the Expert trail?

   The Action: <u>Comparing two groups</u>

   The Operation: <u>Subtraction</u>   Answer: <u>¾ mile longer</u>
                             $(2\frac{1}{4} - 1\frac{1}{2} = \frac{3}{4})$

Additional word problems for Lesson 16 skills practice are on page 98.

Multiply or Divide?

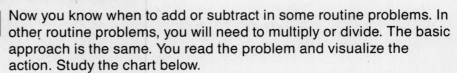

Aim: To understand when to use multiplication and when to use division to solve a word problem

What You Need to Know

Now you know when to add or subtract in some routine problems. In other routine problems, you will need to multiply or divide. The basic approach is the same. You read the problem and visualize the action. Study the chart below.

Choose Multiplication or Division

Action	Operation
Joining equal groups to find a total	Multiplication
Sharing equally to find the size of each group or **Making groups of a given size** to find the number of groups	Division

Think About It

What do you learn when you divide by "sharing equally"?

You learn the size of each group.

What do you learn by "making groups of a given size"?

You learn the number of groups.

Read the problems below. Visualize the action in each.

Example A Skiing lessons cost $15. They are given for groups of 8 people each morning. How much will it cost Marly to take 5 lessons?

The Action: *Joining equal groups*

The Operation: *Multiplication*

The Execution:
$$\begin{array}{r} 15 \\ \times 5 \\ \hline 75 \end{array}$$
Answer: *$75*

Example B There are 57 people waiting for the chairlift. Each chair carries 3 people. How many chairs will be needed to carry all the people?

The Action: *Making groups of a given size*

The Operation: *Division*

The Execution:
$$\begin{array}{r} 19 \\ 3\overline{)57} \end{array}$$
Answer: *19 chairs*

Did you notice the unneeded fact in Example A? Were you able to visualize the action in each problem?

Practice

For each problem, visualize the action described. Then write the action and the answer. (Are you remembering to reword all the questions to yourself?)

1. Small buses take guests from the lodge to the ski lift. Each mini-bus holds 16 riders. How many minibuses are needed to take 80 guests to the ski lift?

   The Action: Making groups of a given size

   The Operation: Division   Answer: 5 buses
                                            (80 ÷ 16 = 5)

2. A toboggan is a long sled without runners. There are 14 tobog-gans available. Each toboggan holds 3 people. How many people can use the toboggans at one time?

   The Action: Joining equal groups

   The Operation: Multiplication   Answer: 42 people
                                            (14 × 3 = 42)

3. Mr. Ewing drove his snowmobile for $2\frac{1}{2}$ hours and traveled 60 miles. What was his average speed in miles per hour?

   The Action: Sharing equally

   The Operation: Division   Answer: 24 miles per hour
                                            (60 ÷ 2½ = 24)

4. The guests at the lodge ordered 5 pizzas and 6 sandwiches from the snack bar. The pizzas cost $7.75 each. How much did the guests spend for the pizzas altogether?

   The Action: Joining equal groups

   The Operation: Multiplication   Answer: $38.75
                                            (7.75 × 5 = 38.75)

5. In one morning, 127 ski-lift tickets were sold. The ticket office col-lected $3,175 for those tickets. What was the cost of each ticket?

   The Action: Sharing equally

   The Operation: Division   Answer: $25.00
                                            (3.175 ÷ 127 = 25)

Additional word problems for Lesson 17 skills practice are on page 99.

39

Lesson
18

Interpret the Remainder

Aim: To show an answer that makes sense when the problem is a quotient with a remainder

What You Need to Know

Often when you divide, you will have a **remainder** in your answer. Suppose you have completed Step 4 (carry out the plan), and you have a remainder. Does it make sense to show that in your answer? To decide, read the problem again. The problem will tell you how to **interpret,** or show, the answer.

The best form for the answer may be one of these:

- the computed mixed-number answer
- the quotient rounded up to the next whole number
- the quotient rounded down to the next whole number
- the remainder by itself

Think About It

Suppose a problem asked for "number of people" as an answer. You computed an answer of $4\frac{1}{4}$. Would you change it? If so, why?

Yes; "number of people" has to be a whole number.

Read each problem below. Notice how the remainder is interpreted in each.

Example Carmen is going to photograph each of the 126 people in her class for the yearbook. She can take 36 pictures with each roll of film.

Each of the following word problems related to the above event has the same execution:

The Execution:

$$\begin{array}{r} 3\ r18,\ or\ 3\frac{1}{2} \\ 36\overline{)126} \end{array}$$

- How many rolls of film will Carmen have to use?
  Answer: $3\frac{1}{2}$ *rolls (show the mixed-number answer)*
- How many rolls should she buy to take the photos?
  Answer: *4 rolls (round up)*
- How many rolls of film will be completely used?
  Answer: *3 rolls (round down)*
- How many pictures will be taken on the fourth roll?
  Answer: *18 pictures (use only the remainder)*

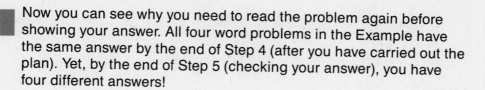

Now you can see why you need to read the problem again before showing your answer. All four word problems in the Example have the same answer by the end of Step 4 (after you have carried out the plan). Yet, by the end of Step 5 (checking your answer), you have four different answers!

Practice

Write the answer to each problem. Also, as shown in the Example, write the way you interpret the remainder in each.

1. There are 75 people waiting to take a minibus tour of the city. Each bus holds 16 people. How many buses are needed for the tour?

   Answer: _5 buses (round up)_   (75 ÷ 16 = 4 r11)

2. The bus makes 4 stops along its 35-mile route. The stops are equally spaced all along the route, with the fourth stop being at the end of the route. How far apart are the stops?

   Answer: _8¾ miles apart (show the mixed number)_   (35 ÷ 4 = 8 r3)

3. Mandy wants to buy postcards of the city. The postcards are $0.15 each. How many postcards can Mandy buy for $1.00?

   Answer: _6 postcards (round down)_   (1.00 ÷ .15 = 6 r10)

4. Thirty-five people want to play soccer. If teams have 11 players each, how many people will be left without a team?

   Answer: _2 people (use only the remainder)_   (35 ÷ 11 = 3 r2)

5. Kevin has a part-time job after school on Mondays and Fridays. He works a total of 11 hours per week. What is the average number of hours he works per day?

   Answer: _5½ hours (show the mixed number)_   (11 ÷ 2 = 5 r1)

Additional word problems for Lesson 18 skills practice are on page 100.

41

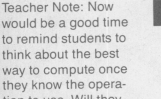

Lesson 19

Cumulative Practice: Choosing the Operation

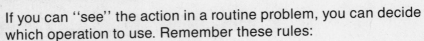

Aim: To decide whether to add, subtract, multiply, or divide to solve a problem

What You Need to Know

Teacher Note: Now would be a good time to remind students to think about the best way to compute once they know the operation to use. Will they compute mentally, use paper and pencil, or use a calculator? For Example A, mental computation would be most efficient. For Example B, paper and pencil or a calculator would be best.

If you can "see" the action in a routine problem, you can decide which operation to use. Remember these rules:

- **Add** to join different-sized groups.
- **Multiply** to join equal groups.
- **Subtract** to separate objects or to compare two groups.
- **Divide** to share equally (find the size of each group) or to make groups of a given size (find the number of groups).

Visualize what is happening in the problem. Then choose the operation that the action suggests.

Think About It

Name the four operations that may be needed in routine problems.

addition, subtraction, multiplication, division

Read the problems below. Think how you would estimate each answer before carrying out the plan.

Example A The Grand Canyon is about 1,740 meters deep measured from the North Rim. It is about 1,370 meters deep measured from the South Rim. About how many meters higher is the North Rim than the South Rim?

The Action: *Comparing two groups*

The Operation: *Subtraction*

The Execution:
$$\begin{array}{r} 1,740 \\ -\ 1,370 \\ \hline 370 \end{array}$$
Answer: *about 370 meters*

Example B During one day, 1,643 people stopped at the Visitor's Center of the park. Suppose the same number of people visited the Center each day in a year. How many people would visit the Center in a year?

The Action: *Joining equal groups*

The Operation: *Multiplication*

The Execution:
$$\begin{array}{r} 1,643 \\ \times\ \ \ 365 \\ \hline 599,695 \end{array}$$
Answer: *599,695 people*

How would you estimate the answers in the Examples? For Example A, you could mentally (in your head) subtract 1,350 from 1,750 and get 400. For Example B, you could multiply 1,600 by 350 and get 460,000. Could you do *that* mentally?

Practice

For each problem, follow all five steps. Remember to visualize the action and to estimate as part of Step 3. Write the action, the operation, and the answer. Be sure to check your answer.

1. Eighteen people want to take a helicopter tour of the Grand Canyon. The helicopter can carry 4 passengers. How many trips must the helicopter make? (Remember to interpret the remainder!)

    The Action: <u>Making groups of a given size</u>

    The Operation: <u>Division</u>   Answer: <u>5 trips</u>
    (18 ÷ 4 = 4.2; round up)

2. Great Smokey Mountains National Park is in North Carolina and Tennessee. The area of the park is about 517,368 acres. There are 273,550 acres of the park in North Carolina. How many acres are in Tennessee?

    The Action: <u>Separating objects</u>

    The Operation: <u>Subtraction</u>   Answer: <u>243,818 acres</u>
    (517,368 ÷ 273,550 = 243,818)

3. In Great Smokey Mountains National Park, there are 170 miles of paved roads. There are 100 miles of gravel roads and 800 miles of horse and foot trails. How many miles of roads and trails are there in the park?

    The Action: <u>Joining different-sized groups</u>

    The Operation: <u>Addition</u>   Answer: <u>1,070 miles</u>
    (170 + 100 + 800 = 1,070)

4. Everglades National Park is about 1,398,937 acres of land and water. About how many square miles is the park?

    The Action: <u>Making groups of a given size</u>

    The Operation: <u>Division</u>   Answer: <u>2,185.8 square miles</u>
    (1,398,937 ÷ 640 = 2,185.8)

5. A 15-mile tram tour operates in the park daily. Mr. and Mrs. Parker bought tram tickets for themselves and their 2 children, who are 7 years old and 4 years old. How much did the Parkers spend on tickets?

    The Action: <u>Joining different-sized groups</u>

    The Operation: <u>Addition</u>   Answer: <u>$10.20</u>
    (4.05 + 4.05 + 2.10 = 10.20)

Teacher Note: Discuss with students the best way to compute each Practice item.
(1: mental; 2: paper and pencil or a calculator; 3: mental; 4: calculator; 5: paper and pencil.)

Tram Tours	
Adult	4.05
Over 62	3.63
Ages 6–12	2.10
Under 6	Free

Additional word problems for Lesson 19 skills practice are on page 101.

Two-Operation Problems

Aim: To solve problems that involve two operations

What You Need to Know

Two operations may be needed to solve a problem. This occurs when the problem has a main question and a "hidden" question.

Step 1: As always, read, reread, and reword. Then decide what the "hidden" question is. Continue by following Steps 2–5 to answer the hidden question.

Step 2: Find the needed facts.   **Step 4:** Carry out the plan.

Step 3: Plan what to do.   **Step 5:** Check the answer.

Now you have answered the hidden question. Repeat Steps 2–5 to answer the main question. In Step 2, one of the needed facts will be the answer to the hidden question.

Think About It

Why do you need to answer the hidden question first?

That answer is part of the data for the main question.

Pro-Photo Film Prices		
Film Size	Film Price	Processing Price
disc	2.59	2.49
110-12	1.99	1.99
110-20	2.59	2.59
135-24	2.89	3.99
135-36	3.35	5.99

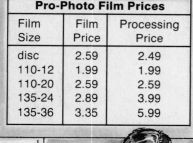

Read each problem below. Notice the order of the operations.

Example A Kevin bought 1 roll of 110-12 film and 3 rolls of 110-20 film. How much did the 4 rolls cost?

Hidden Question: *How much did the 3 rolls of 110-20 film cost?*

First Operation:	Second Operation:	Answer
Multiplication	*Addition*	**to Main**
2.59	7.77	**Question:**
× 3	+ 1.99	$9.76
$7.77	9.76	

Example B Pro-Photo had 165 rolls of 135-36 film. They sold 12 rolls. The rest were sent to their 3 branch stores. Each branch store received the same number of rolls. How many rolls of 135-36 film were sent to each store?

Hidden Question: *How many rolls were left after 12 rolls were sold?*

First Operation:	Second Operation:	Answer
Subtraction	*Division*	**to Main**
165	51	**Question:**
− 12	3)‾153	*51 rolls*
153		*of film*

In Example A, you *multiply* to find the answer to the hidden question. Then you *add* that answer to the cost of one roll of 110-12. This gives you the answer to the main question. In Example B, you *subtract* to answer the hidden question. Then you *divide* that answer to find the answer to the main question.

Practice

For each problem, write the names of the two operations you will use. Then solve the problem. Do not skip any steps!

1. Juanita bought 3 rolls of 135-36 film. She gave the clerk a $20 bill. How much change did she receive?

   First Operation: __Multiply__

   Second Operation: __Subtract__

   Answer:

   $9.95

   (3 × 3.35 = 10.05; 20.00 − 10.05 = 9.95)

2. During a special sale, Pro-Photo sold disc film with processing included for $4.50. How much savings was this over the regular cost of disc film and processing?

   First Operation: __Add__

   Second Operation: __Subtract__

   Answer:

   $0.58

   (2.59 + 2.49 = 5.08; 5.08 − 4.50 = 0.58)

3. During the first day of the sale, the store manager recorded the number of disc films sold by each of her 3 branch stores. They had sold 123 discs, 96 discs, and 84 discs. What was the average number of discs sold by each branch?

   First Operation: __Add__

   Second Operation: __Divide__

   Answer:

   101 discs

   (123 + 96 + 84 = 303; 303 ÷ 3 = 101)

4. Saul paid for the processing of 1 roll of 135-24 film and of 3 disc films. What was his total bill?

   First Operation: __Multiply__

   Second Operation: __Add__

   Answer:

   $11.46

   (3 × 2.49 = 7.47; 7.47 + 3.99 = 11.46)

5. Sally bought a new camera from Pro-Photo for $200. She paid $44 down and agreed to pay the balance in 12 equal payments. How much will Sally pay each month?

   First Operation: __Subtract__

   Second Operation: __Divide__

   Answer:

   $13.00

   (200 − 44 = 156; 156 ÷ 12 = 13)

Teacher Note: Point out to students that the order in which they do the two operations in each problem is important. In Example B, for instance, if they were to divide and then subtract, they would get the wrong answer. (They would get 165 ÷ 3 = 55 and 55 − 12 = 43; 43 rolls.) During discussion of the Practice items, have students state the "hidden" question in each.

Additional word problems for Lesson 20 skills practice are on page 102.

Lesson 21

Choosing a Sensible Answer

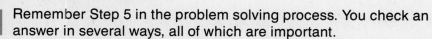

Aim: To choose the most reasonable answer to a problem by using common sense

What You Need to Know

Teacher Note: Examples A and B and all the Practice items are not complete word problems. Too little information is provided for students to find the answers on their own. This has been done in order to focus students' attention on the concept of "sense" in an answer.

Remember Step 5 in the problem solving process. You check an answer in several ways, all of which are important.

- **Think** whether the answer makes sense.
- **Match** the answer with your estimate (made in Step 3).
- **Check** your computation.

Notice that the *first* thing to check is whether the answer makes sense. *Review* the problem and the question. *Visualize* the action in the problem. Is the answer reasonable in view of the whole problem? If not, then something is wrong!

- It may be a poor plan.
- It may be an incorrect computation.
- It may be the wrong label, such as "feet" for "miles."

Checking for sense is easy. It involves no calculation. However, it *can* signal a wrong solution. If your answer is reasonable, there is a good chance that your solution is correct.

Teacher Note: Remind students that once they have checked the reasonableness, or sense, of an answer, they still need to do the checks of matching with estimates and checking calculations. Lesson 22, which follows this lesson, provides more help with estimating.

Think About It

Why is checking the sense of an answer the *first* thing to do for Step 5?

If the answer makes no sense, then you know something is wrong, even

if the computations are done correctly.

Read each Example below. Each one asks a question. Think about each of the four answer choices carefully. The correct answer is circled. Can you see why the other three choices do not make sense?

HEIGHT ?

Example A Marie is in the seventh grade. How old is Marie's younger sister?

(8 yrs. old)   18 yrs. old   28 yrs. old   38 yrs. old

Example B What is the height of a bedroom door?

7 inches   (7 feet)   7 yards   7 miles

In Example A, "8 yrs. old" is the only reasonable answer. A person 18, 28, or 38 years old would be older than a student in the seventh grade. In Example B, you need to focus on the units (inches, feet, yards, miles). Only "7 feet" makes sense.

Practice

For each question, circle the answer that is the most reasonable.

1. The gas tank on Miguel's car is empty. About how many gallons of gasoline will it take to fill the tank?

    0.2 gal.   2 gal.   (20 gal.)   200 gal.

2. Ms. Keyser drove from New York to Los Angeles in 5 days. About how many miles did she drive?

    28 miles   280 miles   (2,800 miles)   28,000 miles

3. Janet took her two sisters to the movies. How much did they spend for three tickets?

    $1.05   ($10.50) $105.00 $1,050.00

Teacher Note: Check that students understand why three of the four answer choices do not make sense in each item. Checking the sense of an answer sometimes requires an experiential background that individual students may not have.

Some students may have no idea, for instance, what a normal car's gas tank holds in gallons. Help students not to worry in such a case. When they can't check the reasonableness of an answer in this way, they can still match with their estimate and check their computation.

4. Rebecca has a pet cat. How much does her cat weigh?

    (8.9 lb.)   89 lb.   8.9 oz.   0.89 oz.

5. It took Kent 15 minutes to jog to Maria's house. How far did Kent jog?

    10 yards   100 yards   (1 mile)   10 miles

Additional word problems for Lesson 21 skills practice are on page 103.

47

Checking Estimates and Computations

Aim: To use estimation and computation checks to judge whether an answer is accurate

What You Need to Know

Teacher Note: Remind students that a computation may check as accurate even if the answer does not make sense. In that case, there is a problem with the unit label or the plan. If the unit label is correct, then students need to do all Steps 1-5 again, rethinking the plan.

Remember, checking an answer is done in stages. First check that the answer makes sense. Then check your computations. Estimating is one check on reasonableness. It also tells you if your computed answer is probably accurate. When you check your computations, do one of the following:

- Add or multiply "backwards" (switch the numbers).
- Subtract to check addition; add to check subtraction.
- Divide to check multiplication; multiply to check division.

Think About It

What are two ways to check your addition?

Add "backwards" or subtract.

Read each problem below. Notice how estimation is used to check for sense. Also notice how the computation is checked.

Example A Carol makes jewelry. She sells one style of earrings for $29.50. The materials cost $10.15. What is the difference between her selling price and her cost of materials?

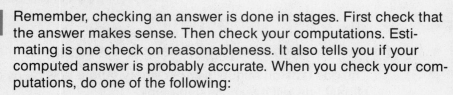

Estimation:	30	**Computation:**	29.50
	$-\,10$		$-\,10.15$
	20		19.35

Estimated Answer: $20.00   **Computed Answer:**

Computation Check: 19.35 $19.35
                                   $+\,10.15$
                                    29.50

Example B Carol sold 22 bracelets to the owner of a gift shop. The owner paid $19.95 for each bracelet. How much money did Carol make on the sale of these bracelets?

Estimation:	20	**Computation:**	19.95
	$\times\,20$		$\times\,22$
	400		438.90

Estimated Answer: $400.00   **Computed Answer:**

Computation Check: 22 $438.90

                     $\times\,19.95$ or   19.95
                       438.90 $22\overline{)438.90}$

In each Example A and B, the estimated answer helps to show that the computed answer is reasonable. The computation check shows that the answer is accurate.

Practice Teacher Note: Students' computation checks may vary from the examples given in the boxes.

Follow all five steps to solve each word problem below. Then write the estimated answer and the computed answer. Show your computation check in the box next to each word problem.

1. Carol bought 11 stones to use in making her jewelry. She paid $54.23 for the stones. What was the average price she paid for each stone?

   Estimated Answer: __$5.00__   Computed Answer: __$4.93__
   (50 ÷ 10 = 5)   (54.23 ÷ 11 = 4.93)

1. Computation Check

$$\begin{array}{r} 4.93 \\ \times 11 \\ \hline 54.23 \end{array}$$

2. To make a 3-string necklace, Carol needs 51 large black beads and 108 small silver beads. How many black beads will she need to make 9 necklaces?

   Estimated Answer: __450 beads__   Computed Answer: __459 beads__
   (50 × 9 = 450)   (51 × 9 = 459)

2. Computation Check

$$\begin{array}{r} 9 \\ \times 51 \\ \hline 459 \end{array} \quad \text{or} \quad \begin{array}{r} 51 \\ 9\overline{)459} \end{array}$$

3. During a craft show, Carol sold 18 pairs of earrings. She made $395.10 altogether on the sale of the earrings. What was the average price of the earrings?

   Estimated Answer: __$20.00__   Computed Answer: __$21.95__
   (400 ÷ 20 = 20)   (395.10 ÷ 18 = 21.95)

3. Computation Check

$$\begin{array}{r} 21.95 \\ \times 18 \\ \hline 395.10 \end{array}$$

4. Bev bought 2 pairs of earrings for $19.95 a pair, a bracelet for $11.25, and 2 necklaces for $10.95 each. How much did Bev spend?

   Estimated Answer: __$70.00__   Computed Answer: __$73.05__
   (20 + 20 + 10 + 10 + 10 = 70)   (19.95 + 19.95 + 11.25 + 10.95 + 10.95 = 73.05)

4. Computation Check

$$\begin{array}{r} 10.95 \\ 10.95 \\ 11.25 \\ 19.95 \\ +\,19.95 \\ \hline 73.05 \end{array}$$

5. It takes 9 inches of silver wire to make a pair of earrings. Carol has 4 feet of silver wire. How many pairs of earrings can she make?

   Estimated Answer: __5 pairs__   Computed Answer: __5 pairs__
   (4 × 12 = 48; 50 ÷ 10 = 5)   (4 × 12 = 48; 48 ÷ 9 = 5 r3, round down)

5. Computation Check

$$\begin{array}{r} 9 \\ \times 5 \\ \hline 45 \end{array} \quad \text{and} \quad \begin{array}{r} 45 \\ +\,3 \\ \hline 48 \end{array}$$

A. On each line, write **T** or **F** to tell whether the statement is true or false.

_T_   1. Real-life problems often include facts that are not needed to solve the problems.

_F_   2. The first thing you should do when you see a diagram is to look for the facts you need to solve the problem.

_F_   3. Tables and charts often make it harder to see patterns in the data.

_T_   4. Pictographs and bar graphs make it easy to see how facts relate to each other.

_T_   5. Routine problems are solved by adding, subtracting, multiplying, or dividing.

_F_   6. To join different-sized groups, you should multiply.

_F_   7. When you divide and there is a remainder in your answer, you should always round up to the next whole number.

_T_   8. In a two-operation problem, you answer the "hidden" question before you answer the main question.

_F_   9. If your answer makes sense and is close to your estimate, your answer must be correct.

_F_   10. You can check subtraction by subtracting "backward."

B. On each line, write the word that best completes the sentence.

data   11. You cannot solve a word problem unless you can find all the needed _____.

appendix   12. The section in the back of this book where general facts are found is called the _____.

addition   13. If the action in a problem describes joining different-sized groups, you would use the operation _____ to solve the problem.

division   14. If the action in a problem describes making groups of a given size to find the number of groups, you would use the operation _____ to solve the problem.

reasonable
(or sensible)   15. When checking your answer in Step 5, the first thing to check is whether the answer is _____.

C. Circle the letter of the correct answer.

16. There are 215 seventh-graders, 277 eighth-graders, and 21 teachers at Adams School. How many students go to Adams School?
   a. 513 students   **b.** 492 students   **c.** 503 students   **d.** 482 students

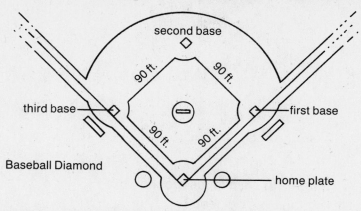

Baseball Diamond

17. Michelle ran from home plate, past first base and second base, to third base. How far did she run?
   a. 270 feet   **b.** 180 feet   **c.** 90 feet   **d.** 360 feet

18. How many more people live in Deville than in Ceville?
   a. 20,914 more people   **c.** 74,862 more people
   b. 24,616 more people   **d.** 16,596 more people

City	Population
Aville	39,364
Beville	24,815
Ceville	29,133
Deville	45,729

Car Sales

19. Five people sold cars in April. They each sold the same number of cars. How many cars did each person sell?
   a. 4 cars   **b.** 5 cars   **c.** 7 cars   **d.** 35 cars

20. Beth walks 1.5 km to school. Ross walks 2.1 km to school. How much farther does Ross walk than Beth?
   a. 3.6 km   **b.** 1.4 km   **c.** 0.6 km   **d.** 3.4 km

21. Sandwiches cost $3.29 at Donna's Deli. How much did Barb pay for 5 sandwiches?
   a. $16.25   **b.** $15.05   **c.** $15.45   **d.** $16.45

22. There are 24 pictures on each roll of film. You are going to take 108 pictures. How many rolls of film should you buy?
   a. 5 rolls   **b.** 4 rolls   **c.** $4\frac{1}{2}$ rolls   **d.** 12 rolls

23. Rachel bought 4 felt-tip markers that cost $0.79 each. She gave the clerk $5.00. How much change did she receive?
   a. $3.16   **b.** $1.84   **c.** $2.16   **d.** $1.94

Go on to the next page.

D. Read and reread each word problem. Then follow the directions to show your solution to the problem.

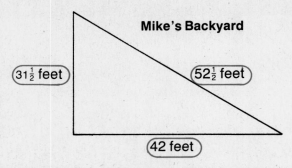

Mike's Backyard

$31\frac{1}{2}$ feet $52\frac{1}{2}$ feet

42 feet

24. This is a diagram of Mike's backyard. Mike wants to put a fence around the outside of his yard. <u>How many feet of fencing does he need?</u>
   a. Underline the question.
   b. Circle the needed facts in the problem.
   c. Describe your plan: <u>Add (length of first side + length of second side +</u>
      length of third side = feet of fencing needed)
   d. If an estimate can be made, show it here: <u>30 + 40 + 50 = 120</u>
   e. Carry out your plan. Answer: <u>126 feet   ($31\frac{1}{2}$ + $52\frac{1}{2}$ + 42 = 126)</u>
   f. Check your answer. If you got an incorrect answer, tell how you know it is wrong. Then write the correct answer.
      <u>Students who got incorrect answers should mention computation error or</u>
      <u>that the answer was not reasonable.</u>

25. There are 312 people going on a field trip to the art museum. Each bus holds 48 people. <u>How many buses are needed to take everyone to the museum?</u>
   a. Underline the question.
   b. Circle the needed facts in the problem.
   c. Describe your plan: <u>Divide and interpret the remainder (number of people</u>
      going on trip ÷ number of people bus holds = number of buses needed)
   d. If an estimate can be made, show it here: <u>300 ÷ 50 = 6</u>
   e. Carry out your plan. Answer: <u>7 buses   (312 ÷ 48 = 6.5; round up)</u>
   f. Check your answer. If you got an incorrect answer, tell how you know it is wrong. Then write the correct answer.
      <u>Students who got incorrect answers should mention computation error or</u>
      <u>that the answer was not reasonable.</u>

3 More Help With Strategies

■ Making a Diagram ■ Making a Table ■ Making an Organized List ■ Cumulative Practice: Diagram, Table, List ■ Finding a Pattern ■ Writing an Equation— Addition or Subtraction ■ Writing an Equation—Multiplication or Division ■ Cumulative Practice: Writing Equations ■ Using a Formula ■ Making a Hard Problem Easier ■ Guessing and Checking ■ Exact or Estimated Answers ■ More Than One Strategy

Lesson 23

Making a Diagram

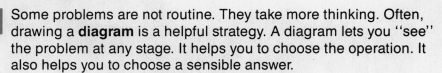

Aim: To solve problems by drawing simple line diagrams

What You Need to Know

Teacher Note: Be sure students understand how the diagram was developed for each Example. Some students may realize, in Example B, that they could multiply 3 times 2 to get the 6. The students who understand this would not need to make the diagram and then count. For most students, however, the tree diagram is a helpful strategy to learn.

Some problems are not routine. They take more thinking. Often, drawing a **diagram** is a helpful strategy. A diagram lets you "see" the problem at any stage. It helps you to choose the operation. It also helps you to choose a sensible answer.

Here is how to plan (Step 3) with a diagram:

- First, draw and label the diagram as clearly as you can.
- Second, reread the problem. Make sure your drawing fits the events. Put as much data on the diagram as you can.
- Third, plan what to do. Think about what the diagram shows you. Think about any other data in the problem.

Think About It

What two things does a diagram help you to choose?

It helps you to choose the operation and a sensible answer.

Study each Example. Notice how the diagram fits the events.

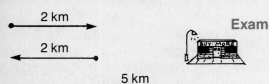

Max's house — 5 km — store

2 km →

← 2 km

5 km →

Example A Max lives 5 km from the store. He jogged 2 km toward the store. Then he remembered that he had left his wallet at home. He jogged back, got his wallet, and jogged to the store. How far did he jog in all?
Strategy: *Make a diagram, then add.*
Answer: *9 km*

Example B Mary has blue shorts, red shorts, and white shorts. She has a green blouse and a yellow blouse. How many different outfits can she make?
Strategy: *Make a diagram, then count.*
Answer: *6 outfits*

Shorts	Shirts	Outfits
b	g	blue and green
	y	blue and yellow
r	g	red and green
	y	red and yellow
w	g	white and green
	y	white and yellow

54

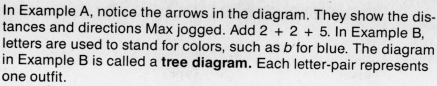
In Example A, notice the arrows in the diagram. They show the distances and directions Max jogged. Add 2 + 2 + 5. In Example B, letters are used to stand for colors, such as *b* for blue. The diagram in Example B is called a **tree diagram.** Each letter-pair represents one outfit.

Teacher Note: Students may need help with Practice item 3. Be sure they understand how the use of directions (such as south) helps them to draw the diagram. Also be sure students understand that two operations are needed.

Practice

For each problem, write the strategy. Draw a diagram in the space provided. Then solve the problem.

1. Jason lives 8 km from the city library. He rode his bike 3 km toward the library before he remembered that his library card was at home. He rode back for the card and then rode to the library. After getting his books, he rode his bike back home. How far did Jason ride in all?

   Strategy: Make a diagram, then add.

   Answer: 22 km (3 + 3 + 8 + 8 = 22)

1. Diagram

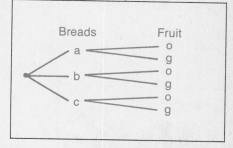

2. Vera can make apple bread, banana bread, and cranberry bread. She also has a pound of oranges and a pound of green grapes. She wants to take one loaf of bread and one type of fruit to a friend. How many pairs of choices does Vera have?

   Strategy: Make a diagram, then count.

   Answer: 6 pairs of choices

2. Diagram

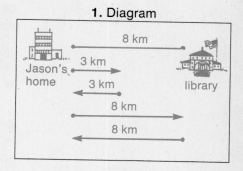

3. Celia walked south 2 km from her house to the market. Next she walked northeast 4 km from the market to Carrie's house. Then she walked back to her own house. Celia walked 9 km in all. How far is it from Celia's house to Carrie's house?

   Strategy: Make a diagram; add and subtract.

   Answer: 3 km (9 − (4 + 2) = 3)

3. Diagram

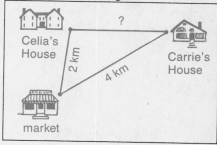

4. Write a word problem of your own. Write a problem that making a diagram would help to solve.

   Answers will vary, but check that making a diagram would indeed help

   to solve the problem. This is a good Practice item around which to hold

   class discussion.

Additional word problems for Lesson 23 skills practice are on page 105.

Making a Ratio Table

Aim: To solve problems by making tables that show how two things change in relation to each other

What You Need to Know

A good way to organize data is to make a **table.** With a table, you can see if there is a pattern in the data. You can also see if any data are missing.

A table is useful when the data form a **ratio** (RAY-she-oh). A ratio is a way of showing how two items are related to each other. The word **rate** is often (though not always) a clue to a ratio problem.

For example, suppose you walk at a rate of 3 miles per hour. That sets up a ratio of 3 to 1 (3 miles to 1 hour). So, if you walk 6 miles, it will take 2 hours. The pattern in the data is 3 to 1, 6 to 2, 9 to 3, and so on. Once you work out the data, put it in a table. Then you can use the table over and over again. You don't have to keep working out the pattern.

Think About It

What is a ratio? What word can be a clue to a ratio problem?

A ratio is a way of showing how two items are related to each other. The

word ''rate'' can be a clue.

Read each problem below. In Example A, you learn that there is a ratio of 16 to 2 (16 tacos in 2 hours). That information is used to begin the table. Notice how the table is labeled, for *Tacos* and *Hours.* Notice, too, how the table has been set up to help answer both questions.

Example A The Pep Club is selling tacos, burritos, juice, peanuts, and popcorn at the school fair. Anita and Jason have sold 16 tacos in 2 hours. At this rate, how many hours will it take them to sell 64 tacos?

Strategy: *Make a ratio table.*

Tacos	16	32	48	64
Hours	2	4	6	8

Answer: *It will take 8 hours to sell 64 tacos.*

Example B How many tacos will Anita and Jason sell in 6 hours?

Strategy: *Check the table already made.*

Answer: *They will sell 48 tacos in 6 hours.*

To extend the table in Example A, add the first number to itself: 16 + 16 = 32 and 2 + 2 = 4. This second entry tells you that 32 tacos would be sold in 4 hours. Then, to each of those numbers (32 and 4), add 16 and 2 again: 32 + 16 = 48 and 4 + 2 = 6. Continue adding the first number to the last number to get the next entry in each row. With the finished table, the pattern is easy to see.

Practice

Solve each problem by making a ratio table. Then write the answer as a complete sentence.

1. Anita uses 4 ounces of meat for every 3 tacos. How many tacos can she make with 20 ounces of meat?

   The Table:

Ounces of meat	4	8	12	16	20
Tacos	3	6	9	12	15

   Answer: She can make 15 tacos with 20 ounces of meat.

2. How many ounces of meat does Anita need to make 12 tacos? (Use the table in Practice item 1.)

   Answer: She needs 16 ounces of meat to make 12 tacos.

3. Jason and Anita sell 2 bags of peanuts for every 3 boxes of popcorn they sell. At this rate, how many boxes of popcorn will they have sold when they have sold 12 bags of peanuts?

   The Table:

Peanuts	2	4	6	8	10	12
Popcorn	3	6	9	12	15	18

   Answer: They will have sold 18 boxes of popcorn.

4. Jason thinks that 3 out of 5 students in his class will buy a taco from him. There are 30 students in his class. How many classmates does Jason expect will buy a taco from him?

   The Table:

Students buying	3	6	9	12	15	18
Students in class	5	10	15	20	25	30

   Answer: He expects 18 students to buy a taco from him.

5. During the last hour, Anita and Jason sold burritos at 3 for $2.00. How many burritos could you buy for $10.00?

   The Table:

Burritos	3	6	9	12	15
Cost	2	4	6	8	10

   Answer: You could buy 15 burritos for $10.

6. Write a word problem of your own. Write a problem that making a ratio table would help to solve.

   Answers will vary, but check that making a ratio table would indeed help to solve

   the problem. This is a good practice item around which to hold class discussion.

Additional word problems for Lesson 24 skills practice are on page 106.

Making an Organized List

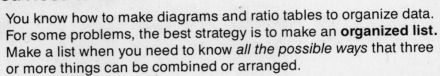

Aim: To solve problems by listing possible outcomes in an orderly way

What You Need to Know

You know how to make diagrams and ratio tables to organize data. For some problems, the best strategy is to make an **organized list.** Make a list when you need to know *all the possible ways* that three or more things can be combined or arranged.

It is important to use an orderly approach when you draw up your list. *Have a system in mind.*

- You might start your list with the lowest number.
- You might start your list with the letter nearest the beginning of the alphabet.

With a system, you can check that you have listed all the possibilities. The problem situation will help you decide on the system. The main thing is to use one that makes sense to you.

Think About It

Why is it good to have a system in mind when you organize a list?

With a system, you can check that none of the possibilities has been left

out by mistake.

Read each problem below. Notice how the lists are organized. Also notice how letters are used in Example B to stand for the names of the people.

Example A How many different 3-digit numbers can you make with the numerals 1, 2, and 3?

Strategy: *Make an organized list.*

123   213   312
132   231   321

Answer: *6 different 3-digit numbers*

Example B Al, Bob, Carl, and Dennis are playing a Ping-Pong match. Each player will play each other player once. How many games will be played?

Strategy: *Make an organized list.*

AB   BC   CD
AC   BD
AD   **Answer:** *6 games*

In Example A, all the numbers that can begin with the numeral 1 are listed first. Then all the numbers that can begin with 2 are listed. The numbers beginning with 3 are listed last. In each column, the numbers are listed in increasing order.

In Example B, letters stand for names. They are listed in alphabetical order. Once game AB is listed, that means Al and Bob have played a game. Remember, each player will play each other player *once.* So, game BA (Bob and Al) is not listed as a different game — it would have the same two players.

Practice

Make an organized list to help you solve each problem. Show your list and the answer. Follow all five problem solving steps.

1. How many different ways can you arrange 3 books on a shelf? (Use A, B, and C to represent the books.)

   Answer: 6 different ways

   1. Organized List

ABC	BAC	CAB
ACB	BCA	CBA

2. How many different 2-digit numbers can you make with the numbers 1, 2, 3, and 4?

   Answer: 12 different 2-digit numbers

   2. Organized List

12	21	31	41
13	23	32	42
14	24	34	43

3. Julie has 5 friends: Ken, Lou, Micky, Nan, and Otto. She wants to invite 2 friends over for dinner. How many different choices does she have?

   Answer: 10 different choices

   3. Organized List

KL	LM	MN	NO
KM	LN	MO	
KN	LO		
KO			

4. Marie has 5 books about horses and 3 books about dogs. How many different ways could she lend 1 book about horses and 1 book about dogs to a friend? (Hint: Label the horse books A, B, C, D, and E. Label the dog books 1, 2, and 3.)

   Answer: 15 different ways

   4. Organized List

A1	B1	C1	D1	E1
A2	B2	C2	D2	E2
A3	B3	C3	D3	E3

5. Write a word problem of your own. Write a problem that making an organized list would help to solve.

   Answers will vary, but check that making an organized list would indeed

   help to solve the problem. This is a good Practice item around which to

   hold class discussion.

Additional word problems for Lesson 25 skills practice are on page 107.

Cumulative Practice —
Diagram, Ratio Table, List

Aim: To decide whether to make a diagram, a ratio table, or an organized list to solve a problem

What You Need to Know

You have learned three strategies for organizing data. These strategies are:

- **Make a diagram** to ''see'' the events in the problem.
- **Make a table** to extend the numbers in a ratio problem.
- **Make an organized list** to find all the ways three or more things can be combined or arranged.

Often, only one of these strategies will work. For some problems, though, two or even all three of these strategies may work. In that case, choose the one that works best for you.

Think About It

Name three strategies you can use to organize data during Step 3 of the problem solving process.

Make a diagram, a table, or an organized list.

Read the problem below. Notice how two different strategies may be used to solve the problem.

Example Eva has three pens. One pen has red ink, one has blue ink, and one has green ink. She has two styles of stationery. One is white paper and one is tan paper. How many different looking, addressed envelopes can Eva mail?

Strategy: *Diagram*

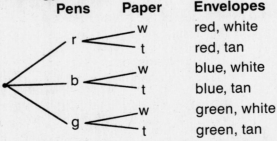

Pens	Paper	Envelopes
r	w	red, white
	t	red, tan
b	w	blue, white
	t	blue, tan
g	w	green, white
	t	green, tan

Strategy: *Organized list*

RW BW GW
RT BT GT

Answer: *6 different looking, addressed envelopes*

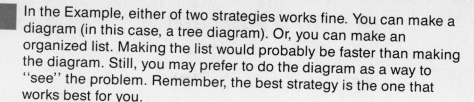

In the Example, either of two strategies works fine. You can make a diagram (in this case, a tree diagram). Or, you can make an organized list. Making the list would probably be faster than making the diagram. Still, you may prefer to do the diagram as a way to ''see'' the problem. Remember, the best strategy is the one that works best for you.

Teacher Note: Accept other strategies students may list in the Practice items if, indeed, those strategies would help them to solve the problems and if they get the right answers.

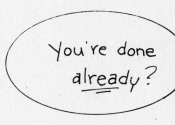

You're done already?

Practice

Follow all five problem solving steps. Then write the name of the strategy you used (diagram, ratio table, or organized list). Write the answer to the problem.

1. How many different ways can Amy, Beth, Joe, and Dan stand in a single line?

   Strategy: Organized list   Answer: 24 ways

2. Albert lives 3 miles from the swimming pool. He walked three-quarters of a mile toward the pool and then remembered that he had forgotten his bathing suit. He walked back home, got his suit, and then walked to the pool. He swam for 1 hour, ate lunch, and walked straight home. How far did Albert walk in all?

   Strategy: Diagram   Answer: 7 miles

3. Fran uses 2 eggs for every 3 cups of flour in her secret recipe. How many eggs will she need if she uses 12 cups of flour?

   Strategy: Ratio table   Answer: 8 eggs

4. Raul is making muffins. He can use wheat or white flour. He can put cranberries, raisins, or nuts in the muffins. How many different kinds of muffins can he make?

   Strategy: Organized list   Answer: 6 kinds of muffins

5. Melissa is decorating a hexagonal (6-sided) tablecloth. She will put 2 blue daisies at each corner. She will put 5 white daisies along each edge. How many daisies will she make in all?

   Strategy: Diagram   Answer: 42 daisies

Additional word problems for Lesson 26 skills practice are on page 108.

Finding a Pattern

Aim: To solve problems that require finding patterns in numbers or in geometric figures

What You Need to Know

Once you organize the data for a word problem, you may find that you need to extend the data. You did this when you made ratio tables. Knowing the first ratio, you were able to extend the table of ratios according to a certain pattern.

A **pattern** can be described by one or more operations. The operation for extending a ratio table is addition. (You added the first ratio to itself to get the next entry. Then you added the first ratio to the second entry to get the third, and so on.)

A **progression** is a kind of pattern. It is a series of numbers or geometric figures. The numbers or figures change step by step, based on a pattern. Once you learn the pattern, you can find the next number or figure that belongs in the series. You may see the word *rate* used with a progression as well as a ratio.

Think About It

Fill in the missing words: A pattern can be described by one or more

_____operations_____. A series of numbers or geometric figures

that change based on a pattern is called a _____progression_____.

Study each Example below. Can you figure out the patterns in the progressions? In Example B, the table is extended after the data are organized.

Example A Continue the pattern in each progression.

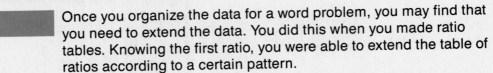

Progression: 1, 4, 7, 10, 13, ____, ____ **Answer:** *16, 19*
Progression: 6, 8, 16, 18, 36, ____, ____ **Answer:** *38, 76*

Progression: △, ▢, ⬠, ⬡, __, __ **Answer:** ⬡, ⬢

Example B It takes Marcos 6 days to paint a fence. He is paid only $1 the first day. He is paid twice as much the second day, and so on, doubling the amount each day. At this rate, how much will Marcos be paid on the sixth day?

Organize the Data:

Day	1	2	3	4	5	6
Pay	1	2	4	8	16	32

Answer: *$32*

In Example A, the pattern in the first progression is +3. The pattern in the second progression is +2, ×2. In the third progression, each figure has one more side than the figure before it. Also, all sides are of equal length. In Example B, a table is used to organize the data. The word problem stated the pattern in the progression for you.

Practice

For items 1-4, continue the pattern in each progression. Write your own progression for item 5. Solve the problems in items 6-8. Organize the data to help you find the pattern in each.

1. 3, 7, 11, 15, 19, __23__, __27__ (+4)

2. 26, 23, 20, 17, 14, __11__, __8__ (−3)

3. 1, 5, 10, 14, 28, __32__, __64__, (+4, ×2)

4.

5. Write a progression of your own here.
   Check that students' answers follow a pattern.
   _____

6. Bacteria (bak-TIR-ee-ah) are single-celled organisms. They reproduce by dividing in two. They may do this every 20 minutes. Starting with one bacterium, how many would there be after 2 hours of cell division?

   Organize the data:

Bacteria	1	2	4	8	16	32
Minutes	20	40	60	80	100	120

   Answer: __32 bacteria__   (The progression for Bacteria is ×2; for Minutes, +20)

7. A caterpillar is crawling up a branch that is 10 feet long. Every day it crawls up 5 feet. Then it slides back 4 feet while sleeping. How many days will it take the caterpillar to reach the end of the branch?
   Organize the data: Use the margin to draw a diagram.

   Answer: __6 days__   (See diagram annotation in margin.)

8. Kerri wants to be paid $1 for the first hour she works. She wants to be paid $4 for the second hour, $9 for the third hour, and so on. At this rate, how much will Kerri earn for the eighth hour?

   Organize the data:

Hour	1	2	3	4	5	6	7	8
Pay	1	4	9	16	25	36	49	64

   Answer: __$64__   (The progression for Hour is +1; for Pay, +3, +5, +7, ...)

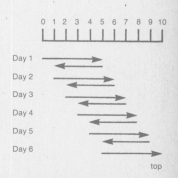

Additional word problems for Lesson 27 skills practice are on page 109.

63

Writing an Equation — Addition or Subtraction

Aim: To solve problems by writing addition or subtraction equations

What You Need to Know

Some problems can be solved with **equations.** An equation shows "real" problem events in a mathematical way. It uses numbers and letters. A letter in an equation is called a **variable.** It stands for an unknown number. That is the information you are looking for.

In this lesson, you will write equations that use addition and subtraction. When writing an equation, do the following:

- First, think what you are looking for. Use a letter (the variable) to stand for it.
- Second, decide which operation to use. Remember, add to join different-sized groups. Subtract to compare two amounts or to find how many are left.
- Third, write the equation and carry out the plan.

Think About It

What does a variable in an equation stand for?

It stands for an unknown number.

Read each Example. The variable is defined. The operation is described by phrases. The phrases are turned into an equation.

Example A Downtown Nursery has 1,500 ivy plants. The nursery sells 975 ivy plants to 113 stores. How many ivy plants do they have left?

Variable: *Let n = the number of ivy plants left*

Think: *total plants − plants sold = plants left*

Equation: $1{,}500 - 975 = n$

Answer: *525 ivy plants*

Example B Ms. Whitehall is buying fertilizer for her lawn. The fertilizer comes in 25-pound bags. She needs $2\frac{1}{4}$ bags for her front lawn and $4\frac{2}{3}$ bags for her back lawn. How many bags of fertilizer should Ms. Whitehall buy?

Variable: *Let n = bags of fertilizer she needs*

Think: *bags for front + bags for back = bags in all*

Equation: $2\frac{1}{4} + 4\frac{2}{3} = n$

Equation Answer: $6\frac{11}{12}$ **Final Answer:** *7 bags*

In each Example, notice how the variable is chosen to stand for the unknown. In Example B, the answer to the equation is not the final answer. Always reread the question! Ms. Whitehall *needs* $6\frac{11}{12}$ bags of fertilizer. She has to *buy* 7 bags.

Practice

For each problem, write what the variable stands for. Then write the equation and solve the problem.

1. The city park gardeners have decided to brighten the park. They plan to use 480 white daisy plants and 240 yellow daisy plants. How many daisy plants will be used in all?

   Variable: Let n = <u>number of daisy plants used in all</u>

   Equation: <u>480 + 240 = n</u>   Answer: <u>720 daisy plants</u>

2. Tammy works 7 hours per day in the greenhouse. She works $4\frac{3}{4}$ hours before lunch. How long does she work after lunch?

   Variable: Let n = <u>number hours Tammy works after lunch</u>

   Equation: <u>$4\frac{3}{4} + n = 7\frac{1}{2}$</u>   Answer: <u>$2\frac{3}{4}$ hours</u>
   (or, $7\frac{1}{2} - 4\frac{3}{4} = n$)

3. Last week, a hanging basket of flowers sold for $10.59. You can save $4.99 if you buy one this week. How much does a hanging basket of flowers cost this week?

   Variable: Let n = <u>number of dollars flowers cost this week</u>

   Equation: <u>n + 4.99 = 10.59</u>   Answer: <u>$5.60</u>
   (or, 10.59 − 4.99 = n)

Moe's home — 6.25 km — shoe store

4. Each afternoon, Moe follows the path shown on the map. He rides his bike 11.5 km to his part-time job at the nursery. How far is it from the shoe store to the nursery?

   Variable: Let n = <u>number of km from shoe store to nursery</u>

   Equation: <u>6.25 + n = 11.5</u>   Answer: <u>5.25 km</u>
   (or, 11.5 − 6.25 = n)

5. Write a word problem of your own. Write a problem that can be solved with an addition or subtraction equation.

   <u>Answers will vary, but check that the problem can be solved by writing</u>
   <u>an addition or subtraction equation. This would be a good item for class</u>
   <u>discussion.</u>

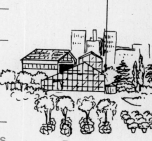

Downtown Nursery

Additional word problems for Lesson 28 skills practice are on page 110.

Lesson 29

Writing an Equation — Multiplication or Division

Aim: To solve problems by writing multiplication or division equations

What You Need to Know

In this lesson, you will write multiplication and division equations. Follow the same basic steps as for writing addition and subtraction equations.

- First, think what you are looking for. Use a letter (the variable) to stand for it.
- Second, decide which operation to use. Multiply to join same-sized groups. Divide to break a group down into smaller groups with the same number in each group.
- Third, write the equation and carry out the plan.

Look at the numbers you are working with. Think about the best method for computing the answer. Can you compute it mentally? Should you use pencil and paper? Or, would a calculator help?

Think About It

What is the only difference in the three steps above from the steps given in Lesson 28?

The only difference is in which operation you might use.

Read each problem. Think about the best method for computing the answer to each equation.

Example A Michael bought 10 times as many tulip bulbs as rose bushes from the Downtown Nursery. He bought 30 tulip bulbs. How many rose bushes did he buy?

Variable: *Let* n = *the number of rose bushes*

Think: *10 x number of bushes = number of tulip bulbs*

Equation: *10 x n = 30*   **Answer:** *3 rose bushes*

Example B At a sale, the nursery owners bought 2,450 evergreen seedlings for $2,192.75. What was the average price they paid for each seedling?

Variable: *Let* n = *average price per seedling*

Think: *total price paid ÷ number of seedlings = average price per seedling*

Equation: *2192.75 ÷ 2450 = n*   **Answer:** *$0.895*

You could solve Example A mentally. A calculator is probably the best way to compute the answer in Example B.

Teacher Note: After students have completed the Practice items, hold a discussion about the best computation method for each item 1-4.
1. paper and pencil; 2. calculator; 3. mentally (or paper and pencil or calculator); 4. calculator.

Practice

For each problem, write what the variable stands for. Then write the equation and solve the problem. Try using the best computation method (mental math, paper and pencil, or calculator) to solve each problem. Remember to check your answers!

1. Marie bought an apple tree and a peach tree. She paid $16.54 for the peach tree. This is twice the amount she paid for the apple tree. How much did she pay for the apple tree?

   Variable: Let n = <u>number of dollars for apple tree</u>

   Equation: <u>2 × n = 16.54</u>   Answer: <u>$8.27</u>

2. Miss Suez spent $41.85 for rose bushes and $13.95 for tomato plants. The amount she spent for rose bushes is how many times greater than the amount she spent for tomato plants?

   Variable: Let n = <u>the number of times greater</u>

   Equation: <u>13.95 × n = 41.85</u>   Answer: <u>3 times</u>

3. The area of each greenhouse at the nursery is 2,500 square feet. There are 2 greenhouses used for vegetable seedlings. How many square feet of space are used for those seedlings?

   Variable: Let n = <u>number of square feet for veg. seedlings</u>

   Equation: <u>2,500 × 2½ = n</u>   Answer: <u>6,250 square feet</u>

4. Fred has 25,000 square feet of lawn to fertilize. Each bag of fertilizer covers 3,500 square feet. How many bags of fertilizer does Fred need to buy? (Hint: The Downtown Nursery sells only full bags of fertilizer.)

   Variable: Let n = <u>number of bags Fred needs</u>

   Equation: <u>25,000 ÷ 3,500 = n</u>   Answer: <u>8 bags</u>
   (Computed answer = 7.14)

5. Write a word problem of your own. Write a problem that can be solved with a multiplication or division equation.

   <u>Answers will vary, but check that the problem can be solved by writing a</u>

   <u>multiplication or division equation. This would be a good item for class</u>

   <u>discussion.</u>

Additional word problems for Lesson 29 skills practice are on page 111.

Cumulative Practice — Writing Equations

Aim: To solve problems by writing addition, subtraction, multiplication, or division equations

What You Need to Know

When you write an equation to solve a problem, think about the "action" shown in the problem. This will help you to choose the right operation. Look at the chart in the Appendix on page 121. It lists, in one place, the actions that tell whether you should add, subtract, multiply, or divide. Use that chart if you need help solving the problems in this lesson.

Often, more than one equation may work. For example, the same problem might be solved by any one of these four equations:

$$1 + n = 4 \qquad n + 1 = 4 \qquad 4 - n = 1 \qquad 4 - 1 = n$$

When you have a choice, just write the equation that makes the most sense to you.

Once you have computed an answer, don't forget to CHECK that answer. Does it make sense? Is it close to your estimate? Is the computation correct?

Think About It

Suppose a problem could be solved by using the equation $6 \div n = 3$. Write two other equations that could be used to solve the same problem.

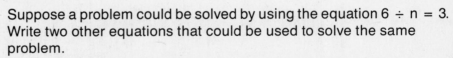
Students should write two of these equations: $3 \times n = 6$, $n \times 3 = 6$,

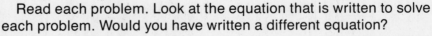
$n = 6 \div 3$.

Read each problem. Look at the equation that is written to solve each problem. Would you have written a different equation?

Example A Elaine and Ruth own a pet shop. Last week Elaine worked 46 hours in the shop. That was twice as many hours as Ruth worked. How many hours did Ruth work?
Variable: *Let n = number of hours Ruth worked*
Equation: $2 \times n = 46$ **Answer:** *23 hours*

Example B Four bags of gerbil food weigh 15.2 kg. If all the bags weigh the same, how much does each bag weigh?
Variable: *Let n = weight of each bag*
Equation: $15.2 \div 4 = n$ **Answer:** *3.8 kg*

Teacher Note: This lesson reassures students that sometimes different equations can be written to solve the same problem. At the same time, depending on your class, you may want to point out that as you carry out the plan for solving an equation, the aim is to get the variable (n) alone on one side of the equal sign. Then the operation that will actually be computed is on the other side.

The equation shown in Example A is $2 \times n = 46$. The problem could also be solved by writing the division equation $46 \div 2 = n$. For the problem in Example B, you could write the multiplication equation $4 \times n = 15.2$.

Practice

Teacher Note: Sample equations are given in the answers to the Practice items. Students might choose to write other equations that are also correct.

For each problem, write what the variable stands for. Then write the equation and solve the problem. Be sure to check each answer. (Are you remembering to follow all five steps?)

1. Rick and Chris work part-time at the pet shop. Last week Rick worked 5 hours more than Chris. If Rick worked 21 hours, how many hours did Chris work?

   Variable: Let n = <u>number of hours Chris worked</u>

   Equation: <u>$n + 5 = 21$</u>   Answer: <u>16 hours</u>

2. Mrs. Peron spent $11.95 on food and toys for her pet collie. She had $47.15 left in her purse. How much money did Mrs. Peron have before she made her purchases at the pet store?

   Variable: Let n = <u>number of dollars before the purchases</u>

   Equation: <u>$n - 11.95 = 47.15$</u>   Answer: <u>$59.10</u>

3. Mr. Avery spent $35.60 for 8 tropical fish. What was the average price of the fish?

   Variable: Let n = <u>average price of fish</u>

   Equation: <u>$35.60 \div 8 = n$</u>   Answer: <u>$4.45</u>

4. Elaine ordered 3 cartons of bird seed. Each carton held the same number of boxes of bird seed. There are 144 boxes of bird seed in all. How many boxes are in each carton?

   Variable: Let n = <u>number of boxes in each carton</u>

   Equation: <u>$3 \times n = 144$</u>   Answer: <u>48 boxes</u>

5. Write a problem about a pet shop that can be solved by writing an equation.

   <u>Answers will vary, but check that the problem can be solved by writing an equation. This would be a good item for discussion.</u>

Additional word problems for Lesson 30 skills practice are on page 112.

Using a Formula

Aim: To solve problems by using formulas

What You Need to Know

You know that when you write an equation, you use a letter (such as *n*) as a variable. It stands for an unknown amount. That is the number you are looking for.

Formulas are special kinds of equations. The same formula may be used with different word problems that have similar situations. When you use a formula—

- first replace any known variables with the numbers they stand for;
- then do the arithmetic to learn the value of the unknown variable.

Study the chart at the left. It shows the formulas that you will use to solve problems in this lesson. Also look at page 122 in the Appendix. For each formula, the Appendix shows the geometric figure and the meanings of the letters.

Some Formulas

Perimeter (P)
(the distance around a figure)
square $P = 4s$
rectangle $P = 2l + 2w$

Circumference (C)
(the distance around a circle)
circle $C = \pi d$
   or $C = 2\pi r$

Area (A)
(the number of square units enclosed by the figure)
square $A = s^2$
rectangle $A = lw$
parallelogram $A = bh$
triangle $A = \frac{1}{2}bh$
circle $A = \pi r^2$

Think About It

How is a formula a special form of equation?

A formula is an equation that can be applied to many word problems.

The values of the variables are all that change.

Read each problem below. Notice the formula that is chosen to solve each.

Example A   The diagram shows the dimensions of Sarah's room. She is putting new carpet on the floor. How many square feet of carpet will she need?

14 ft.

12 ft.

Formula: $A = lw$
Replacing Known Variables: $A = 14 \times 12$
Answer: *168 square feet*

Example B   How many feet of baseboard go around Sarah's room?
Formula: $P = 2l + 2w$
Replacing Known Variables: $P = (2 \times 14) + (2 \times 12)$
Answer: *52 feet*

The floor in Sarah's room is a rectangle. The question in Example A asks for an answer in "square feet." This means that you are looking for an *area*. So, to solve Example A, use the formula for finding the area of a rectangle. To solve Example B, use the formula for finding the *perimeter* of a rectangle.

Practice

For each problem, use the formulas in the chart on page 70. Use the value 3.14 for π. Write the formula and then the answer to the problem. Don't forget to do all five problem solving steps.

On one wall in her room, Sarah painted the geometric shapes shown at the right.

1. Find the area of the circle.

    Formula: $A = \pi r^2$ Answer: 28.26 square feet

2. Find the area of the triangle.

    Formula: $A = \frac{1}{2}bh$ Answer: 30 square feet

3. Find the area of the parallelogram.

    Formula: $A = bh$ Answer: 14 square feet

4. Find the area of the square.

    Formula: $A = s^2$ Answer: 1 square foot

5. Find the perimeter of the square.

    Formula: $P = 4s$ Answer: 4 feet

6. Sarah will bind the edge of a round rug. The diameter of the rug is 3 meters. How many meters of binding does she need?

    Formula: $C = \pi d$ Answer: 9.42 meters

7. There are 4 windows in Sarah's room. Each is 2 meters long and 1.5 meters wide. How many square meters of window space are in the room? (Hint: Find the area of one window and multiply it by the number of windows.)

    Formula: $A = lw$ Answer: 12 square meters

8. Write a problem about your classroom that can be solved by writing a formula.

    Answers will vary, but check that a formula will indeed help to solve

    the problem. This is a good Practice item for class discussion.

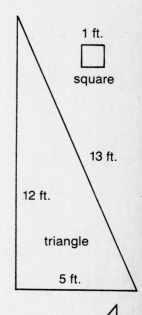

1 ft.
square

13 ft.

12 ft.

triangle

5 ft.

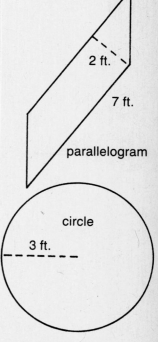

2 ft.

7 ft.

parallelogram

circle

3 ft.

Making a Hard Problem Easier

Aim: To use simpler numbers in order to decide which operations to use

What You Need to Know

Some problems have complex data. Some have complex situations. When you hit a problem that seems too hard, set it aside for a minute. Think up a similar, simpler problem. Think up a situation that is more familiar. Or, think up easier numbers. This will help you to decide which operations to use.

Then think about your plan for solving the *easier* problem. Apply the same plan to the original, complex problem.

This is a tough word problem. I know nothing about "quarks"!

Think About It

Which of these number pairs is simpler: 164 and 33, or 10 and 5?

The number pair 10 and 5 is simpler.

Read each Example below. Notice how the numbers are made simpler before the operation (underlined) is chosen.

Example A The Brookside School had a track-and-field day. Team A ran the 800-meter relay in 3 minutes 29 seconds. Team B took 17 seconds longer to run the same relay. How long did Team B take to run the relay?

To simplify, think: *Suppose Team A took 1 minute and Team B took 30 seconds more. To get Team B's time, I would add 1 minute plus 30 seconds.*

Execution: 3 min. 29 sec.   **Answer:** 3 min. 46 sec.
  + ____ 17 sec.
  3 min. 46 sec.

Just pretend the problem is about atoms.

Example B A local sports store donated 73 tee-shirts to the members of the track-and-field teams. The tee-shirts cost the store $2.79 each. How much did it cost the store to supply the tee-shirts?

To simplify, think: *Suppose the store supplied 10 tee-shirts that cost $2 each. Then I would multiply $2 times 10 to get the total cost.*

Execution: 2.79   **Answer:** $203.67
  × __ 73
  203.67

In each Example, simpler numbers make it easier to picture the "action." Seeing the action, you can decide which operation to use. Then use that operation to solve the original problem.

Teacher Note: Example simplifications are given for the Practice items. Students will simplify with a variety of numbers. Check that students have underlined the planned operation, that it is the correct one, and that the Answers are complete with unit labels.

Practice

Write how you would simplify each problem. Underline the word that gives the operation (as in the Examples). Write the answer to the original problem. Remember to reread the question!

1. In a training session, Gus ran $10\frac{7}{8}$ laps of the track. Mark ran $1\frac{3}{4}$ fewer laps. How many laps did Mark run?

   To simplify, think: Suppose Gus ran 10 laps. Suppose Mark ran 2

   fewer laps. Then I would subtract 2 from 10 to learn how many laps

   Mark ran.

   Answer: $9\frac{1}{8}$ laps $(10\frac{7}{8} - 1\frac{3}{4} = 9\frac{1}{8})$

2. Jody ran $12\frac{1}{2}$ laps while Becky ran 5 laps. How many times farther did Jody run than Becky?

   To simplify, think: Suppose Jody ran 10 laps and Becky ran 5 laps.

   I would divide 10 by 5 to learn how many times farther Jody ran

   than Becky.

   Answer: $2\frac{1}{2}$ times farther $(12\frac{1}{2} \div 5 = 2\frac{1}{2})$

3. Robert is in training for long-distance running. He ran 1.75 hours Monday, 1.5 hours Tuesday, 2.25 hours Wednesday, and 0.75 hour Thursday. His goal is to run 7 hours each week. How many more hours does he need to run to meet his goal?

   To simplify, think: Suppose Robert ran 1 hour each day for four days

   and his goal was 5 hours. Then, to learn the hours left to run, I would

   add the hours already run and subtract the total from 5.

   Answer: 0.75 hour more $(7 - (1.75 + 1.5 + 2.25 + 0.75) = 0.75)$

4. Write a problem of your own. Write one that someone could solve by thinking about a simpler, but similar, problem.

   Answers will vary. Check that the problem includes "complex"

   numbers. This would be a good Practice item for class discussion.

Additional word problems for Lesson 32 skills practice are on page 114.

73

Guessing and Checking

Aim: To solve problems by making a good guess, checking the guess, and then revising it based on the outcome

What You Need to Know

When no other strategy seems to work, there's one more to try — **guess and check.** You learned a little about this strategy back in Unit 1. When you *guess,* you are choosing a trial answer. This trial answer should make sense in terms of the facts you have. Then you use the data in the problem to *check* your guess.

The result of each check gives you a basis for changing your latest guess. Always keep a record of your guesses. This will help you to make more accurate changes.

Think About It

Suppose your first check says your guess was too low. Would you make your second guess higher or lower than your first guess?

You would make your second guess higher.

Read each problem. Notice how each guess is checked.

Example A The sum of two numbers is 38. The difference between the two numbers is 16. What are the two numbers?

Guess: *20 and 18*   **Check:** *Sum is 38; difference is 2. The difference is too small.*

Guess: *30 and 8*   **Check:** *Sum is 38; difference is 22. The difference is too large.*

Guess: *27 and 11*   **Check:** *Sum is 38; difference is 16. The third guess is correct.*

Example B Together, Marcos and Jenny spent $14 at the museum store. Marcos spent $5 more than Jenny. How much did Jenny spend?

Guess: *$4*   **Check:** *If Jenny spent $4, then Marcos spent $9 ($5 more than Jenny). The total is $13. This is less than $14, and so the first guess of $4 is too low.*

Guess: *$5*   **Check:** *If Jenny spent $5 and Marcos spent $10, the total is $15. This is more than $14. So, the second guess of $5 is too high.*

Guess: *$4.50*   **Check:** *If Jenny spent $4.50 and Marcos spent $9.50, the total is $14. The third guess is correct.*

In each Example, the result of the first guess leads the way to the second guess. *Both* the first guess and the second guess lead the way to the third guess.

> Teacher Note: Sometimes, though not often, students' first guess may prove to be the correct answer. In this case, only one guess will be listed for the "Guesses" in the Practice item.

Practice

Use the guess-and-check strategy to solve each problem. Record each guess on the line provided. Circle the final guess, the one that finally proves to be correct. Add unit labels if needed.

1. The sum of two numbers is 44. One number is three times the other number. What are the two numbers?

   Guesses: The correct answer is 11 and 33.

   _____

2. The number has two digits. The sum of the digits is 5. If the digits are reversed, the new number is 9 less than the first number. What is the number?

   Guesses: The correct answer is 32.

   _____

3. Sara sells dinosaur models at the science museum. During the first hour she sold 74 models. She sold 12 more large models than small models. How many of each size model did Sara sell?

   Guesses: The correct answer is 43 large models and 31 small models.

   _____

Science Museum Admissions	
Adults	$3.50
Children	$2.00

4. The Johnsons bought 5 admission tickets to the science museum. They spent $13. How many adults' tickets and how many children's tickets did they buy?

   Guesses: The correct answer is 2 adults' tickets and

   3 children's tickets.

5. Write a word problem of your own that can be solved by guessing and checking.

   Answers will vary, but check that the guess-and-check strategy would

   indeed help to solve the problem. This would be a good Practice item

   for class discussion.

Additional word problems for Lesson 33 skills practice are on page 115.

Exact or Estimated Answers

Aim: To decide which problems can be solved by finding estimated rather than exact answers

What You Need to Know

Suppose you were to ask a friend how much money he or she was carrying right now. Your friend might say something like, "Oh, about 5 dollars." People use estimated numbers a lot. Use an estimated answer when you *cannot get* (impossible) or *do not need* (unnecessary) an exact, computed answer.

- **Impossible:** How many Frisbees will the store sell next year? How many trees are in a forest?
- **Unnecessary:** About how far is it from New York to Los Angeles? Do I have enough money to see the movie?

Before you solve a word problem, think about the kind of answer it requires. Do you need an exact answer? Or, will an estimate be enough?

Think About It

Write a question for which an exact answer would be impossible.

Example: How many fish are in the sea?

Read each problem. Notice whether an exact or estimated answer is used to solve the problem.

Example A   Fran wrote a check to pay for 2 books and 3 felt-tip markers. The books cost $3.95 each. The markers cost $0.89 each. What was the amount of Fran's check?

Exact or estimated? *exact*

Execution:

$$\begin{array}{ccc} 3.95 & .89 & 7.90 \\ \underline{\times\ 2} & \underline{\times\ 3} & \underline{+\ 2.67} \\ 7.90 & 2.67 & 10.57 \end{array}$$

Answer: *$10.57*

Example B   Clay has $20. He wants to buy 2 books that cost $4.95 each. He also wants to buy 4 pens that cost $1.09 each. Does he have enough money to buy everything?

Exact or estimated? *estimated*

Execution:

$$\begin{array}{ccc} 5 & 1 & 10 \\ \underline{\times 2} & \underline{\times 4} & \underline{+\ 4} \\ 10 & 4 & 14 \end{array}$$

Answer: *Yes, Clay has enough money.*

In Example A, Fran had to pay an exact amount for the items she bought. So, an exact, computed answer is necessary. In Example B, you do not need to know the exact cost of the items Clay is buying in order to know if he has enough money.

Practice

For each problem, first decide whether an exact or an estimated answer is necessary. Then solve the problem.

1. Doris promised to work at least 20 hours per week in the stationery store. This week, she worked 5 hours on Monday, 4 hours on Wednesday, $4\frac{3}{4}$ hours on Friday, and $8\frac{1}{3}$ hours on Saturday. Did Doris work as many hours as she promised?

   Exact or estimated? <u>estimated</u>   Answer: <u>Yes, she did.</u>

   $(5 + 5 + 5 + 8 = 23)$

Sal's Stationery Summer Sale

	Were	Now
Calendars	$3.95	$1.49
Scribble Pads	$1.89	$0.56
Address Books	$4.95	$2.59

2. Lizzie bought 1 calendar and 2 address books. She gave the clerk the correct amount. How much did she give the clerk?

   Exact or estimated? <u>exact</u>   Answer: <u>$6.67</u>

   $(1 \times 1.49) + (2 \times 2.59) = 6.67$

3. Sal needs at least 200 different kinds of greeting cards to fill his new card rack. He ordered 92 different birthday cards. He also ordered 79 different get-well cards. Will Sal have enough cards to fill his new rack?

   Exact or estimated? <u>estimated</u>   Answer: <u>No, he will not.</u>

   $(90 + 80 = 170)$

4. Roberto bought 10 greeting cards for $0.75 each. He gave the clerk $20. How much change did he receive?

   Exact or estimated? <u>exact</u>   Answer: <u>$12.50</u>

   $(20.00 - (10 \times 0.75) = 12.50)$

5. Write a word problem of your own that can be solved by finding an estimated answer.

   <u>Answers will vary, but check that an exact answer would be either</u>

   <u>impossible or unnecessary. This would be a good Practice item for</u>

   <u>class discussion.</u>

Additional word problems for Lesson 34 skills practice are on page 116.

77

Lesson 35

More Than One Strategy

Aim: To recognize that more than one strategy often may be used for solving a word problem

What You Need to Know

In this unit you have learned many strategies for solving word problems. Think what you have learned about each of these:

- **diagrams** (to "see" the action)
- **tables** (for ratios and other patterns)
- **organized lists** (to cover all possible answers)
- **equations and formulas** (for problems with variables)
- **guess and check** (making more and more accurate guesses)
- **simplifying hard problems** (using easier numbers)

Sometimes you will know right away which method will work *best*. Or, you may see a *choice* of strategies, where two or three different ones can each solve the same problem. Or, you may want to use a *combination* of strategies. Sometimes you won't be sure what to do! If one strategy leads to a "dead end," try a different strategy.

Think About It

Where can you look for a formula outside the problem?

You can look in the Appendix (or in Lesson 31).

Read each problem. Notice how two strategies may be used.

Example A Joe has 8 more tennis balls than Rob. Together they have 24 tennis balls. How many does Rob have?

Strategy: *guess and check (using organized list)*

Execution:

Rob's	Joe's	Total
3	11	14
6	14	20
8	16	24

Answer: *8 tennis balls*

Example B Kim rode her bike 4 km from her house to the gym. Then she rode $3\frac{1}{2}$ km from the gym to the park and then back to her house. The total trip was 10 km. How far did Kim ride from the park back to her house?

Strategies: *diagram and equation*

Execution: $3\frac{1}{2} + 4 + n = 18$

Answer: $2\frac{1}{2}$ *km*

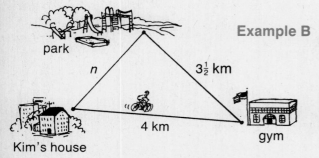

park

n

$3\frac{1}{2}$ km

4 km

gym

Kim's house

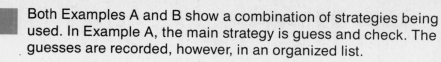

Both Examples A and B show a combination of strategies being used. In Example A, the main strategy is guess and check. The guesses are recorded, however, in an organized list.

In Example B, the main strategy is an equation. The diagram will not give you the answer, as some diagrams do. But it does help you to visualize the problem.

Practice

For each problem, follow all five problem solving steps. Then write the name of the strategy you used, and write the answer. (Remember, often more than one strategy will work. Try the strategy that makes the most sense to you.)

1. Jean wants to paint her bedroom, which is 10 feet long and 9 feet wide. She can use gray or ivory paint for the woodwork. She can use yellow, green, or blue paint for the walls. How many different ways can Jean paint her bedroom?

   Strategy: diagram (or   Answer: 6 different ways
   organized list)

2. Brian is saving money to buy a radio. He saved 1 cent the first day, twice as much the second day, and so on, doubling the amount each day. If this pattern continues, how much will Brian have saved on the seventh day?

   Strategy: table for pattern   Answer: $1.27

   (1 + 2 + 4 + 8 + 16 + 32 + 64 = 127)

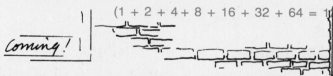

Coming!

3. The Parkers bought 6 movie tickets and spent $19. How many adults' tickets and how many children's tickets did they buy?

   Strategy: guess and check (may   Answer: 2 adults', 4 children's
   be in organized list)

4. Jose bought seventeen 1-kg boxes of bird seed. He paid $35.87. How much does a 1-kg box of bird seed cost?

   Strategy: simplify (or equation)   Answer: $2.11

   (35.87 ÷ 17 = 2.11)

5. Roxanne is tiling the floor of her hallway with 1-foot square tiles. The hallway is 4 feet wide and 8 feet long. How many tiles will she need?

   Strategy: formula (or diagram)   Answer: 32 tiles

   (4 × 8 = 32)

6. Tonya has four stuffed animals. She has an elephant, a giraffe, a monkey, and a zebra. In how many different ways can she arrange them in a straight line?

   Strategy: organized list   Answer: 24 different ways

Movie Tickets
Adults $4.50
Children   2.50

EGMZ GEMZ MEGZ ZEGM
EGZM GEZM MEZG ZEMG
EMGZ GMEZ MGEZ ZGEM
EMZG GMZE MGZE ZGME
EZGM GZEM MZEG ZMEG
EZMG GZME MZGE ZMGE

Unit 3 Review

A. On each line, write **T** or **F** to tell whether the statement is true or false.

T   1. Drawing a diagram for a word problem can help you "see" the problem, choose the operation, and decide if your answer makes sense.

F   2. Use a formula when you need to know all the possible ways that three or more things can be combined or arranged.

T   3. Three strategies that help you to organize data are making a diagram, making a ratio table, and making an organized list.

F   4. All word problems can be solved with equations.

F   5. Using a calculator is the best way to solve any word problem.

T   6. Thinking about the action in a word problem can help you to choose the operation.

F   7. There is only one correct equation that can be used to solve a problem.

T   8. If a problem seems difficult, it often helps to think about a similar but simpler problem.

T   9. When you use the guess-and-check strategy, you use the data in the problem to check your guess.

F   10. There is always one best strategy to use to solve a word problem.

B. On each line, write the word that best completes the sentence.

ratio   11. A pair of numbers that describes a rate or comparison is called a _____.

progression   12. A _____ is a series of numbers or geometric figures that change according to a pattern.

variable   13. A letter in an equation that stands for an unknown number is called a _____.

formula   14. A special equation with more than one variable but only one unknown is called a _____.

estimated   15. When it is either unnecessary or impossible to find an exact answer to a word problem, you can use an _____ answer.

C. Circle the letter of the correct answer.

16. Lara lives 5 km from school. One morning, she rode her bike 2 km before she remembered that she forgot her homework. She rode back home for her homework and then rode to school. How far did Lara ride her bike that morning?

  a. 7 km   **b.** 10 km   **c.** 9 km   **d.** 14 km

17. Max thinks that 3 out of 5 students in his class will go to the class skating party. There are 35 students in his class. How many classmates does Max expect to go to the skating party?

  a. 15 students   **b.** 21 students   **c.** 25 students   **d.** 18 students

18. How many different ways can you arrange 3 cereal boxes on a shelf?

  a. 6 different ways   **c.** 9 different ways
  b. 3 different ways   **d.** 12 different ways

19. What is the next number in this progression? 1, 5, 9, 13, 17, _____

  a. 18   **b.** 19   **c.** 20   **d.** 21

20. Next week, 3 new players will join the soccer team. This will bring the total number of players to 21. How many players are on the team now?

  a. 24 players   **b.** 18 players   **c.** 17 players   **d.** 22 players

21. Steve has 3 times as many balls as bats. He has 12 balls. How many bats does he have?

  a. 4 bats   **b.** 15 bats   **c.** 36 bats   **d.** 9 bats

22. A rectangular bedroom is 12 feet long and 15 feet wide. How much carpet is needed to cover the floor?

  a. 180 square yards   **c.** 180 square feet
  b. 180 feet   **d.** 180 yards

23. Sara read $37\frac{1}{2}$ pages while Bret read 15 pages. How many times more pages did Sara read than Bret?

  a. 2 times more   **c.** $2\frac{1}{2}$ times more
  b. $3\frac{1}{2}$ times more   **d.** 3 times more

24. The sum of two numbers is 25. The product of the two numbers (one times the other) is 154. What are the two numbers?

  a. 5 and 5   **b.** 11 and 14   **c.** 10 and 15   **d.** 7 and 22

25. Ed drove 309.4 miles on Monday, 593.2 miles on Tuesday, 487.9 miles on Wednesday, and 212.4 miles on Thursday. About how many miles did he drive in all?

  a. about 1,500 miles   **c.** about 1,700 miles
  b. about 1,400 miles   **d.** about 1,600 miles

Go on to the next page.

Unit 3 Review (Continued)

D. Read and reread each word problem. Then follow the directions to show your solution to the problem.

26. Pete is painting a room. On the walls, he can use (blue paint, yellow paint, or green paint.) On the ceiling, he can use (white paint) or (pink paint.) <u>How many different ways can he paint the room?</u>

Walls		Ceiling	
b		w	b, w
		p	b, p
y		w	y, w
		p	y, p
g		w	g, w
		p	g, p

    a. Underline the question.

    b. Circle the needed facts in the problem.

    c. Describe your plan: <u>Make a diagram, then count.</u>

    d. If an estimate can be made, show it here: <u>cannot be made</u>

    e. Carry out your plan. Answer: <u>6 ways</u>

    f. Check your answer. If you got an incorrect answer, tell how you know it is wrong. Then write the correct answer.

        Students who got incorrect answers should mention computation error or

        that the answer was not reasonable.

27. Barb took ($15.23) from her wallet to buy groceries. She then had ($31.15) left in her wallet. <u>How much money did Barb have in her wallet before she bought her groceries?</u>

    a. Underline the question.

    b. Circle the needed facts in the problem.

    c. Describe your plan: <u>Write an equation. Let n = money in wallet before she bought groceries; n − 15.23 = 31.15; n = 15.23 + 31.15</u>

    d. If an estimate can be made, show it here: <u>15 + 30 = 45</u>

    e. Carry out your plan. Answer: <u>$46.38</u>

    f. Check your answer. If you got an incorrect answer, tell how you know it is wrong. Then write the correct answer.

        Students who got incorrect answers should mention computation error or

        that the answer was not reasonable.

Step One: Read the Problem

(pages 2–3)

Reword the question in each of the following word problems.

1. There are 27 students in Nicky's class. Each student gives a 5-minute book report. How long does it take to give all the book reports?

   The Question: How many minutes will it take for 27 book reports?

   _____ (135 minutes)

2. Nine students will give reports on Monday. Six students will give reports on Tuesday. How many reports will be given on Monday and Tuesday?

   The Question: What is the total number of reports that will be given on Monday

   and Tuesday?   (15 reports)

3. There are 12 book reports to be given in 3 days. If the same number of reports is given each day, how many reports will be given each day?

   The Question: How many reports will be given in each of 3 days?

   _____ (4 reports)

4. Nicky is going to read a 375-page novel. She plans to read 75 pages each day. How many days will it take her to read the whole book?

   The Question: How many days will Nicky spend reading the book?

   _____ (5 days)

5. Mel read 65 pages each day. She finished her book in 4 days. How many pages were in her book?

   The Question: How long was Mel's book?

   _____ (260 pages)

6. Glen spent $5\frac{1}{2}$ hours working on his report. Jenny spent $7\frac{1}{4}$ hours working on her report. What was the difference in the amount of time the two students spent working on their reports?

   The Question: How much longer did Jenny spend working on her report than

   Glen spent?   ($1\frac{3}{4}$ hours)

7. Twenty-one students read nonfiction books. One-third of these students read biographies. How many students read biographies?

   The Question: How many of the 21 students read biographies?

   _____ (7 students)

Step Two: Find the Facts
(pages 4–5)

Garage Sale	
Friday	10 A.M. – 4 P.M.
Saturday	9 A.M. – 5 P.M.

All books	$ .50
All records	$ .75
All tapes	$1.25

Write only the facts you need to solve each word problem. Use the information in the word problem. Use the facts on the signs if you need them.

1. The Ross family had a garage sale. On Friday, 93 people came to the sale. On Saturday, 126 people came to the sale. How many people came to the sale on the two days?

   The Facts: Number of people on Friday: 93

   Number of people on Saturday: 126   (219 people)

2. Nancy, Sara, and Steve took turns working at the garage sale while it was open on Friday. They each worked the same number of hours. How many hours did each work?

   The Facts: Hours open on Friday: 10 A.M.–4 P.M.

   Number of people working: 3   (2 hours)

3. Kate bought 3 records at the sale. How much did she pay for the records?

   The Facts: Cost of each record: $ .75

   Number of records: 3   ($2.25)

4. Chuck bought 1 book and 1 tape at the sale. How much did he spend on these two items?

   The Facts: Cost of 1 book: $ .50

   Cost of 1 tape: $1.25   ($1.75)

5. Jean spent $4.50 on records. How many records did she buy?

   The Facts: Money spent: $4.50

   Cost of each record: $ .75   (6 records)

6. Casey bought a skateboard for $10.50 and a pair of roller skates for $5.75. How much more did he spend for the skateboard than the roller skates?

   The Facts: Cost of skateboard: $10.50

   Cost of roller skates: $5.75   ($4.75)

7. Bev bought four games for $5.00. She paid the same for each game. How much did each game cost?

   The Facts: Total cost of games: $5.00

   Number of games: 4   ($1.25)

Cumulative Practice: Steps 1 and 2

(pages 6–7)

For each work problem below, underline the question and circle the facts needed to solve the problem.

1. Carrie has been playing the flute in the Adams Junior High Band for 2 years. She played in 14 concerts last year and 17 concerts this year. In how many concerts has she played in the last 2 years? (31 concerts)

Ace Music Store

$4\frac{1}{2}$ blocks   7 blocks

Carrie's house   Kim's house

2. Every Saturday, Carrie walks from her house to the Ace Music Store for her flute lesson. After her lesson, she walks back home. How far does she walk in all to and from her lesson? (9 blocks)

3. How much farther from Ace Music does Kim live than Carrie? (2½ blocks)

4. Carrie practices the flute for 30 minutes each day. How many minutes does she practice in a week? (210 minutes)

5. Kris plays a drum in the band. On Monday, he practiced for 15 minutes. On Tuesday, he practiced 3 times as long as he did on Monday. How long did he practice on Tuesday? (45 minutes)

6. Kris is learning 3 new musical pieces. He is planning to practice for 1 hour and will spend equal amounts of time practicing each new piece. How long will he practice each new piece? (20 minutes)

7. There are 29 students in the brass section of the band. If 21 of these students play trumpets, how many play other brass instruments? (8 students)

8. The Boyers bought 4 adult tickets to the Fall Concert. How much did they spend? ($5.00)

Fall Concert	
adults	$1.25
students	$ .50

9. The Slaters bought only adult tickets. They spent $6.25. How many tickets did they buy? (5 tickets)

10. There were 2 parts to the concert. The first part took 25 minutes. The second part took 35 minutes. It was 75 minutes from the beginning to the end of the concert. How long was the intermission? (15 minutes)

Step Three: Plan What to Do

(pages 8–9)

Write a plan for solving each problem. Label the plan. Outline it in parentheses. Then show how you would compute an estimate based on your plan.

1. Amy works on the Highland School newspaper. On Monday, she spent 28 minutes writing an editorial. She took 11 minutes to type it and 20 minutes to proofread it. How many minutes did she spend working on the editorial?

   The Plan: <u>Add   (minutes writing + minutes typing + minutes proofreading = total minutes)</u>

   The Estimate: <u>30 + 10 + 20 = 60   (59 minutes)</u>

2. Before writing a story, Paul spent 3 days interviewing 18 students. He interviewed the same number of students each day. How many students were interviewed each day?

   The Plan: <u>Divide   (total number of students interviewed ÷ number of days = number of students interviewed each day)</u>

   The Estimate: <u>18 ÷ 3 = 6   (6 students)</u>

3. Eighteen editions of the newspaper are published during the school year. There are 3 sports reporters who work on the paper. If each sports reporter writes a story for each edition of the paper, how many sports stories will be written during the school year?

   The Plan: <u>Multiply   (number of editions × number of reporters = number of stories)</u>

   The Estimate: <u>20 × 3 = 60   (54 stories)</u>

4. There 21 boys, 15 girls, and 3 teachers who work on the newspaper. How many more boys than girls work on the paper?

   The Plan: <u>Subtract   (number of boys − number of girls = how many more boys)</u>

   The Estimate: <u>20 − 15 = 5   (6 boys)</u>

5. Five students distributed the newspapers to 35 classrooms. Each student went to the same number of classrooms. To how many classrooms did each of the five students go?

   The Plan: <u>Divide   (number of classrooms ÷ number of students = number of classrooms each student went to)</u>

   The Estimate: <u>35 ÷ 5 = 7   (7 classrooms)</u>

6. Mark and Todd wrote lead stories for the newspaper 13 times last year. Mark wrote the lead story 5 more times than Todd did. How many times did each person write the lead story?

   The Plan: <u>Guess and check</u>

   The Estimate: <u>cannot be made   (Mark wrote 9; Todd wrote 4)</u>

Teacher Note:
Although students are
not asked to solve the
Practice items, the
answers are provided
for your information.
Accept reasonable
estimates.

Cumulative Practice: Steps 1, 2, and 3
(pages 10–11)

For each word problem below, <u>underline</u> the question. (Circle) the needed facts.
Then write your plan and your estimate.

Rainbow Car Wash	
Wash	
car	($3.00)
van	$3.50
truck	$4.00
Wax	($2.25)
Vacuum	$1.25

Students should circle
$3.00 as a needed
fact for items 1 and 2,
and $2.25 for item 1.

1. Tony had his car washed and waxed. <u>How much was his bill?</u>

   The Plan: _____Add_____ (price of car wash + price of wax = total price)

   The Estimate: _____3 + 2 = 5_____ ($5.25)

2. On Monday, (17 cars,) 6 vans, and 2 trucks were washed in 1 hour. <u>How much did the car wash earn during this hour?</u>

   The Plan: _____Multiply_____ (number of cars × price of washing car = total earned on washing cars)

   The Estimate: _____20 × 3 = 60_____ ($51)

3. It takes (60 minutes) for (20 cars) to go through the car wash. <u>How long does it take for 1 car to go through the car wash?</u>

   The Plan: _____Divide_____ (total number of minutes ÷ number of cars = number of minutes for one car)

   The Estimate: _____60 ÷ 20 = 3_____ (3 minutes)

4. During one day, (124 cars,) (49 vans,) and 38 trucks were washed at the Rainbow Car Wash. <u>How many more cars than vans were washed?</u>

   The Plan: _____Subtract_____ (number of cars − number of vans = difference between cars and vans)

   The Estimate: _____120 − 50 = 70_____ (75 cars)

5. Kelly works at the car wash (7½ hours) a day. One week she worked (4 days.) <u>How many hours did she work that week?</u>

   The Plan: _____Multiply_____ (number of hours worked in 1 day × number of days worked = total number of hours worked)

   The Estimate: _____8 × 4 = 32_____ (30 hours)

6. It takes about (50 gallons) of water to wash one car. If (124 cars) are washed, <u>about how many gallons of water are used?</u>

   The Plan: _____Multiply_____ (number of cars × number of gallons per car = total number of gallons)

   The Estimate: _____120 × 50 = 6000_____ (6,200 gallons)

7. One day, (51 vehicles) were vacuumed. (Three people) vacuumed the vehicles. If each person vacuumed the same number of vehicles, <u>how many vehicles did each person vacuum?</u>

   The Plan: _____Divide_____ (total number of vehicles ÷ number of people = number of vehicles per person)

   The Estimate: _____60 ÷ 3 = 20_____ (17 vehicles)

Step Four: Carry Out the Plan

(pages 12–13)

Show your answer to each problem.

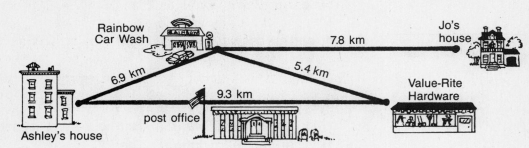

15.6 km

12.3 km

0.9 km

$60

342 gallons

30 colors

5 packages

7½ hours

6 pounds

$4.24

$18.78

$34.20

15 cartons

1. On Tuesday, Jo drove a round trip from her house to the Rainbow Car Wash. How far did she drive?

2. On Monday, Ashley drove from her house to the Rainbow Car Wash and then to Value-Rite Hardware. How far did she drive in all?

3. On Saturday, Ashley left her house at 1 P.M. Jo left her house at 2 P.M. They both drove directly to the Rainbow Car Wash. How much farther did Jo drive than Ashley?

4. The Value-Rite Hardware sells paint for $12 a gallon. How much do 5 gallons of paint cost?

5. One week, Tim sold 123 gallons of indoor paint, 219 gallons of outdoor paint, and 117 gallons of stain. How many gallons of paint did he sell that week?

6. The paint-color display has 6 rows of colors. There are 5 different colors in each row. How many paint colors are in the display?

7. Lori needs 20 new hinges for some cabinet doors. There are 4 hinges in each package. How many packages should Lori buy?

8. Hector worked in the hardware store for $2\frac{1}{2}$ hours on Monday. On Tuesday, he worked three times as many hours. How long did he work on Tuesday?

9. Joy bought $3\frac{1}{2}$ pounds of roofing nails and $2\frac{1}{2}$ pounds of finishing nails How many pounds of nails did she buy?

10. Garden tools are on sale at Value-Rite Hardware. A shovel that usually costs $12.99 is on sale for $8.75. How much do you save if you buy the shovel on sale?

11. Stacy bought a rake for $7.99 and a sprinkler for $10.79. How much did she spend in all?

12. A hand saw costs $20.79. An electric circular saw costs $54.99. How much more does the electric saw cost than the hand saw?

13. Leo wants to order 360 quarts of oil for the hardware store. There are 24 quarts of oil in a carton. How many cartons of oil should he order?

Cumulative Practice: Steps 1, 2, 3, and 4
(pages 14–15)

For each problem, underline the question and circle the needed facts. Then think about your plan and make a mental estimate. Write your answer on the line.

13 gallons

1. Jack's aquarium holds 18 gallons of water. Each week he replaces 5 gallons of the water with fresh water. <u>How many gallons of water are not replaced each week?</u>

$16.75

2. Grace bought 5 new fish for her aquarium. Each fish cost $3.35. <u>How much did she pay for the 5 new fish?</u>

$11.45

3. Tim bought plants for $3.95 and gravel for $7.50. <u>How much did he spend for the plants and gravel?</u>

19 guppies

4. Megan bought 8 guppies for her aquarium. Several weeks later, she counted 27 guppies in the aquarium. <u>How many guppies were born in her aquarium?</u>

21 angelfish

5. The Fish Shop had 126 angelfish in 6 aquariums. The same number of fish were in each aquarium. <u>How many angelfish were in each aquarium?</u>

18 aquariums

6. There are 54 aquariums along one wall in the Fish Shop. The aquariums are arranged in 3 rows. Each row has the same number. <u>How many aquariums are in each row?</u>

880 boxes

7. One week the Fish Shop sold 110 boxes of fish food. If the same number of boxes were sold each week, <u>how many would be sold in 8 weeks?</u>

206 people

8. During the Saturday Sale at the Fish Shop, 325 people came into the shop. There were 119 people who made purchases. <u>How many people came into the shop and did not make a purchase?</u>

$1,190

9. If the 119 people who made purchases spent an average of $10 each, <u>how much money was taken in at the Fish Shop during the Saturday Sale?</u>

122 customers

10. On Monday, Pete helped 57 customers before lunch and 65 customers after lunch. On Tuesday, he helped 40 customers before lunch and 36 customers after lunch. <u>How many customers did Pete help on Monday?</u>

Step Five: Check the Answer

(pages 16–17)

For each problem, use the two-part check to decide if the computed answer is a correct answer. If it is not, correct it.

Starbrite Roller Rink Admission	
adults	$3.25
children under 12	$1.75

1. How much more is the admission to Starbrite Roller Rink for an adult than for a child?

   The Execution: $3.25   Computed Answer: $1.40
   $$\begin{array}{r} \$3.25 \\ -\ 1.75 \\ \hline \$1.40 \end{array}$$
   The correct answer is $1.50.

   The Check: _____

2. Children's admissions to Starbrite Roller Rink on Saturday totaled $525. How many children skated there on Saturday?

   The Execution: 300.   Computed Answer: 300 children
   $$1.75\overline{)52500.}$$
   $$\underline{525}$$
   $$0$$
   The given answer of 300 children is correct.

   The Check: _____

3. During the first hour of skating, three videos were played. Each video lasted $1\frac{1}{4}$ minutes. How long did the three videos last?

   The Execution: $3 \times \frac{5}{4} = \frac{15}{12} = 1\frac{1}{4}$ Computed Answer: $1\frac{1}{4}$ minutes
   The correct answer is 3¾ minutes.

   The Check: _____

4. Skates are stored on shelves in the skate room. On one wall there are 6 shelves. There is room for 48 pairs of skates on each shelf. How many pairs of skates can be stored along this wall?

   The Execution: 8   Computed Answer: 8 pairs of skates
   $$6\overline{)48}$$
   The correct answer is 288 pairs of skates.

   The Check: _____

5. There were 32 girls and 24 boys who took part in the skating races. How many more girls than boys raced?

   The Execution: 32   Computed Answer: 56 more girls
   $$\begin{array}{r} 32 \\ +\ 24 \\ \hline 56 \end{array}$$
   The correct answer is 8 more girls.

   The Check: _____

6. Phil skated around the rink 5 times before he stopped for a snack. He skated forward $1\frac{3}{4}$ times around the rink and backward the rest of the time. How many times did he skate around the rink backward?

   The Execution: $5 - 1\frac{3}{4} = 3\frac{1}{4}$ Computed Answer: $3\frac{1}{4}$ times
   The given answer of 3¼ times is correct.

   The Check: _____

Cumulative Practice: Steps 1, 2, 3, 4, and 5

(pages 18–19)

For each problem, underline the question and circle the needed facts. Think about your plan and make a mental estimate, then write your answer on the line. Don't forget to check each answer.

106 points

1. In a basketball game, the Jets scored 57 points in the first half and 49 points in the second half. The Rams made 19 free throws. How many points did the Jets score in the whole game?

22 free throws

2. The Rams attempted 41 free throws. They made 19 free throws. How many free throws did they miss?

15 points

3. Kathi scored 75 points in 5 basketball games. What was the average number of points she scored in each game?

40 games

4. During the hockey season, the Eagles won 27 games, tied 4 games, and lost 9 games. How many games did they play in all?

169 shots on goal

5. Ivan took 212 shots on goal during the season. He scored 43 goals. How many shots on goal did not score?

$750

6. Each adult paid $3.75 to watch the Eagles play the Blazers. If 200 adults attended the game, how much was collected in adult admissions?

$2.25

7. Max paid $13.50 for 6 children to watch the game. How much did each child's ticket cost?

47 hits

8. Gina and Carol played on the Blue Sox softball team. Gina came to bat 48 times and made 19 hits. Carol came to bat 72 times and made 28 hits. How many hits did the two girls make in all?

162.1 seconds

9. In a track relay, Paul ran the first leg in 46.3 seconds. Sam ran the second leg in 39.4 seconds. Pete ran the third leg in 37.9 seconds. Jeff ran the last leg in 38.5 seconds. How long did it take the boys to run the relay?

28 minutes

10. In practice, Tina jogged once around the track in 5.6 minutes. If she jogged at this same pace, how long would it take her to go around the track 5 times?

Too Much Information

(pages 24–25)

Solve each problem. Be careful to use only the needed facts.

Bowling Scores

	Game 1	Game 2	Game 3
Jean	106	95	117
Lou	96	118	114
Marge	89	125	123

214 pins
_____

1. What was Lou's total score for his first two games?

328 pins
_____

2. What was Lou's total score for all three games?

6 pins
_____

3. How much greater was Marge's score for Game 3 than Jean's score for Game 3?

98 pins
_____

4. Sue and Tim also bowled 3 games each. Sue's total score for the 3 games was 294. Tim's total score was 348. What was Sue's average score for each game?

35 pins
_____

5. Mel had a score of 124 for Game 1. How much greater was Mel's score for Game 1 than Marge's score for Game 1?

1¼ pounds
_____

6. Lou's bowling ball weighs 14 pounds. Marge's bowling ball weighs $15\frac{1}{4}$ pounds. Jean's bowling ball weighs $13\frac{1}{2}$ pounds. How much heavier is Marge's bowling ball than Lou's bowling ball?

160 pounds
_____

7. There were 8 bowling balls on the top storage rack. Each ball weighed 15 pounds. On the bottom rack there were 10 bowling balls that each weighed 16 pounds. What was the total weight of the bowling balls on the bottom rack?

$4.95
_____

8. It cost $1.05 to rent bowling shoes and $1.65 to bowl each game at Ten Pin Lanes. How much did Marge pay to play 3 games if she wore her own shoes?

$0.79
_____

9. After the game, Jean spent $2.37 for 3 lemonades. Lou spent $2.70 for 3 boxes of popcorn. How much did each lemonade cost?

$0.85
_____

10. Ten Pin Lanes has a Saturday Special from 9 A.M.–6 P.M. You can bowl 3 games for $2.55. How much does it cost to bowl a game during the Saturday Special?

Too Little Information

(pages 26–27)

There is not enough information given to solve these problems. Describe the information you need.

1. The Milton School is holding a jog-a-thon to raise money for the computer fund. There is some money in the computer fund now. If $1,500 is raised at the jog-a-thon, how much money will be in the fund in all?

   how much money is in the computer fund now

2. Aaron had a pledge of $0.65 for each time he jogged around the $\frac{1}{4}$-mile track. He jogged around the track for $2\frac{1}{2}$ hours. How much money did Aaron raise?

   how many times Aaron jogged around the track

3. Sherri collected pledges from 7 different people. Each pledged the same amount. What was the total amount pledged for each time Sherri jogged around the track?

   how much each of the 7 people pledged

4. Janet received 14 more pledges than Lynn. How many pledges did Lynn receive?

   number of pledges Janet received or total number of pledges they both received

5. Julie jogged around the $\frac{1}{4}$-mile track for 45 minutes. How many miles did she jog in all?

   how long it took her to jog around once or how many times she jogged around the track

6. Matt has saved some money to buy new shoes for the jog-a-thon. The shoes he wants cost $16.95. How much more money does he need?

   how much money he has saved

7. Nathan and some of his friends jogged a total of 84 times around the track. Each one went around the track the same number of times. How many times around the track did each one jog?

   how many friends jogged

8. The Sport Center will donate a shirt for each person who runs in the jog-a-thon. Each shirt will cost the Sport Center $1.75. How much will it cost them to donate the shirts?

   how many shirts they are donating

9. There were 325 boys and girls who jogged. There were more boys than girls who jogged. How many boys jogged?

   how many more boys than girls jogged

Reading a Diagram
(pages 28–29)

Solve each problem. Use the diagram on page 28 for Problems 1–3.

14.7 km

0.2 km

10.4 km

1. Jesse rode his bike from his house past the swimming pool to Michael's house and then to the fire station. How far did he ride in all?

2. How much farther is it from Jesse's house to the library than it is from the fire station to the library?

3. Michael walked from his house to the fire station and then back home. How far did did he walk?

Use the diagram on page 29 for Problems 4 and 5.

2¾ miles

1¾ miles

4. One morning Julie jogged to Debbie's house. Then she walked the rest of the way along the path until she got back home. How far did she walk that morning?

5. After school, Debbie walked the long way to Julie's house. Then together they jogged the short way back to Debbie's house. How far did each girl jog?

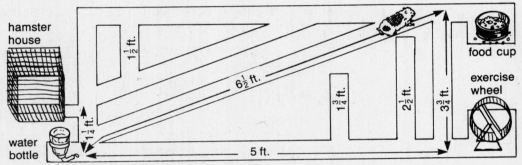

3 hours

15½ feet

45 feet

3¼ feet

1½ feet

6. It took Kim 18 hours to make this maze for her pet hamster. She worked on the maze for the same number of hours a day for 6 days. How many hours did she work on the maze each day?

7. Kim watched the hamster walk from the house to the water bottle to the food cup and then back to the house along the same path. How far did the hamster walk?

8. During one hour, the hamster made 6 trips from the exercise wheel to the food cup and back to the exercise wheel. How far did the hamster walk during that hour?

9. The hamster found the shortest path from the water bottle to the food cup. It walked $\frac{1}{2}$ the distance from the water bottle to the food cup and then turned around. How far did the hamster walk before it turned around?

10. How much farther is it from the water bottle to the food cup than from the water bottle to the exercise wheel?

Reading a Table

(pages 30–31)

Solve each problem. Use the table on page 30 for Problems 1–4.

<u>69,572 more take-offs and landings</u>

1. How many more take-offs and landings were there at Chicago O'Hare International in 1984 than in 1983?

<u>293,576 fewer take-offs and landings</u>

2. In 1984, how many fewer take-offs and landings took place at St. Louis International than at Atlanta International?

<u>871,404 take-offs and landings</u>

3. What was the total number of take-offs and landings at Long Beach in 1983 and 1984?

<u>55,977 take-offs and landings</u>

4. What was the average number of take-offs and landings per month at Chicago O'Hare International in 1983?

Use the table on page 31 for Problems 5 and 6.

<u>615,890 people</u>

5. By how much did Chicago's population decrease between 1950 and 1980?

<u>2,864,371 people</u>

6. By how much did Los Angeles increase in population between 1900 and 1980?

Precipitation

City	Normal Annual Precipitation (in inches)	1984 Precipitation (in inches)
Atlanta, Georgia	48.61	55.39
Boston, Massachusetts	43.84	50.24
Chicago, Illinois	33.34	34.00
Detroit, Michigan	30.97	26.27
Houston, Texas	44.76	48.18
Los Angeles, California	14.85	7.81
New York, New York	42.82	48.19

<u>47.58 inches</u>

7. How many more inches of precipitation were recorded in Atlanta than in Los Angeles in 1984?

<u>4.7 inches</u>

8. How many fewer inches of precipitation than normal were recorded in Detroit in 1984?

<u>3.73 inches</u>

9. Based on the normal annual precipitation, what is the average precipitation in Houston each month?

<u>175.36 inches</u>

10. Based on the normal annual precipitation, what would you expect the total precipitation in Boston to be in the next 4 years?

Reading a Graph

(pages 32–33)

Solve each problem. Use the pictograph on page 32 for Problems 1–3.

325 cans

1. About how many cans have been collected by Mr. Rubin's and Mr. Sewel's classes together?

125 fewer cans

2. About how many fewer cans were collected by Mr. Moy's class than by Mrs. Garcia's class?

750 cans

3. Suppose Ms. Allen's class collects 3 times the number of cans they have now by the end of the month. How many cans will they have by the end of the month?

Use the bar graph on page 33 for Problems 4–6.

about 20 pounds

4. There are 35 students in Mr. Sewel's class. Suppose each student collected the same amount of newspaper. About how many pounds did each student collect?

about 50 pounds

5. About how many more pounds of paper did Ms. Allen's class collect than Mr. Moy's class?

about 2,650 pounds

6. About how many pounds of newspaper were collected by all 5 classes?

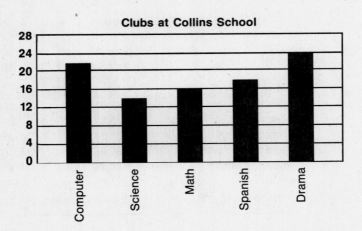

30 members

7. How many members are there in the Science and Math Clubs together?

10 more members

8. How many more members are there in the Drama Club than the Science Club?

44 members

9. If the number of members in the Computer Club doubles by the end of the year, how many members will there be at the end of the year?

12 members

10. If $\frac{2}{3}$ of the members of the Spanish Club attended the last meeting, how many members were at the last meeting?

Using the Appendix

(pages 34–35)

Solve each problem. Use the facts in the Appendix if you need help.

5,000 pounds

1. A pickup truck weighs $2\frac{1}{2}$ tons. How many pounds does the truck weigh?

48 quarts

2. An aquarium holds 12 gallons of water. How many quarts of water does it hold?

2,700 meters

3. Lupe jogs 2.7 kilometers each morning. How many meters does she jog each morning?

576 square inches

4. The area of a table top is 4 square feet. How many square inches is the table top?

1,600 acres

5. City College owns $2\frac{1}{2}$ square miles of land. How many acres does it own?

3¾ quarts

6. There are 5 people in the Agnew family. Each person drinks 3 cups of milk a day. How many quarts of milk do the Agnews drink in a day?

15,000 m²

7. A developer owns a lot with an area of 2.5 hectares. She sells 1 hectare. How many square meters does she still own?

1½ pounds

8. Ron's recipe for macaroni and cheese calls for 8 ounces of cheese. Ron wants to triple the recipe. How many pounds of cheese does he need?

about 500 nails

9. A nail has a mass of 6.5 grams. A box of these nails has a mass of 3.25 kilograms. About how many nails are in the box?

4 gallons

10. Milt is painting 6 rooms in his house. He needs $2\frac{2}{3}$ quarts of paint for each room. How many gallons of paint does he need?

2 pounds

11. You need only one regular stamp on a first-class letter if the letter does not weigh more than 1 ounce. If you had 32 stamps, what is the maximum number of pounds of letters you could mail first class?

1,440 minutes

12. How many minutes are there in a day?

442 weeks

13. Jan's dog is $8\frac{1}{2}$ years old. How many weeks old is her dog?

Add or Subtract?

(pages 36–37)

Solve each problem. Visualize the action to decide which operation you should use.

473 people
_____

8 plant exhibits
_____

447 cars
_____

44 more people
_____

$1.75
_____

$29.99
_____

$4.05
_____

$17.00 more
_____

3¾ hours
_____

10½ pages
_____

5 hours
_____

1 more student
_____

1. On Thursday, 187 adults and 286 children entered the Science Museum. How many people entered the museum on Thursday?

2. Last year, 23 new exhibits of animals or plants were prepared for the museum. If 15 of the exhibits were of animals, how many were of plants?

3. There are 2 parking lots for the museum. The north lot has room for 260 cars. The south lot has room for 187 cars. How many cars can be parked in the two parking lots at one time?

4. A movie about the planets is being shown in the museum's Little Theater. The theater seats 129 people. If 85 people are already seated in the theater, how many more people can be seated?

5. Admission to the museum is $5.25 for adults, $3.50 for children ages 5–16, and free for children under 5. How much more does it cost for an adult to enter the museum than for a 10-year-old child?

6. In the museum gift shop, Dana bought a book about insects for $6.95, an ant farm for $21.75, and a ring for $1.29. How much did he spend in all?

7. Sara bought a book about the planets for $5.95. She gave the clerk $10.00. How much change did she receive?

8. A hardcover book about animals costs $25.95. The same book with a soft cover costs $8.95. How much more does the hardcover book cost?

9. Phil wrote a science report for school. He spent $1\frac{1}{2}$ hours in the library on Monday and $2\frac{1}{4}$ hours in the library on Tuesday. How long was he in the library on Monday and Tuesday?

10. Phil planned to write a 25-page report. He wrote $14\frac{1}{2}$ pages while he was at the library. How many more pages did he have to write at home?

11. Phil spent $1\frac{3}{4}$ hours writing more of his report at home on Monday. He spent another $1\frac{3}{4}$ hours at home on Thursday and $1\frac{1}{2}$ hours on Friday. How many hours did Phil spend writing his report at home?

12. Of the 28 students in Phil's class, he was one of 6 to earn A's on their science reports. Of the rest, 8 students received B's, 10 received C's, 3 received D's, and 1 student received an incomplete. How many more students received an A or a B than received a C or a D?

Multiply or Divide?

(pages 38–39)

Solve each problem. Visualize the action to decide which operation you should use.

1,575 stamps
_____

1. A stamp dealer sold 9 sets of stamps. Each set contained 175 stamps. How many stamps did the dealer sell?

210 stamps
_____

2. Beth's stamp album has 6 pages for Canadian stamps. There are 5 pages for British stamps. Each page holds 35 stamps. How many Canadian stamps does the album hold?

9 stamps
_____

3. Lyle bought 36 stamps from 4 different countries. He bought the same number of stamps from each country. How many stamps did he buy from each country?

35 sets
_____

4. A stamp dealer is packaging stamps in sets of 18 stamps. She has 630 stamps. How many sets may she make?

501 foreign stamps
_____

5. Beth has 167 foreign stamps in her collection. Gina has 3 times as many foreign stamps as Beth has. How many foreign stamps does Gina have?

$10.00
_____

6. Gina bought 8 stamps for her collection. Each stamp cost $1.25. How much did she pay for the 8 stamps?

$2.29
_____

7. Luther spent $13.74 to buy 6 new stamps for his collection. All the stamps cost the same amount. How much did he spend for each stamp?

150 U.S. stamps
_____

8. Candy has 60 foreign stamps. She has $2\frac{1}{2}$ times as many United States stamps as foreign stamps. How many United States stamps does Candy have?

12 inches
_____

9. Some stamps are $\frac{3}{4}$-inch wide. Candy puts 16 of these stamps in a row. How long is the row of stamps?

$1\frac{1}{2}$ inches
_____

10. Pablo wants to put 7 stamps in a row on 1 page in his album. The page is $10\frac{1}{2}$ inches wide. How much room is there for each stamp?

Interpret the Remainder

(pages 40–41)

Solve each problem. Remember to interpret the remainder correctly.

33 seats
(round up)

1. At the carnival, 97 people are waiting to ride the Ferris wheel. Each seat holds 3 people. How many seats are needed?

7 times
(round down)

2. Mike has 38 tickets. How many times may he ride the roller coaster if each ride costs 5 tickets?

6 throws
(round down)

3. At the dart toss, one throw costs $0.15. How many throws does Mai Ling get for $0.95?

7½ hours
(mixed number)

4. Ed works at the ticket booth 4 days a week. He works a total of 30 hours per week. What is the average number of hours he works per day?

2 tickets
(remainder)

5. Donna has 26 tickets. The Whirley Bird ride costs 6 tickets. Donna rides as many times as she can. How many tickets does she have left?

21 boxes
(round up)

6. The snack bar sells bags of peanuts. There are 24 bags of peanuts packaged per box. How many boxes are needed to have at least 500 bags of peanuts at the snack bar?

36 tickets
(round down)

7. Marta has $5.50. How many $0.15 tickets can she buy?

$0.10
(remainder)

8. Phil has $4.90. How much money will he have left if he buys all the $0.15 tickets he can?

9⅗ turns
(mixed number)

9. The Ferris wheel makes 1 complete turn every 25 seconds. If the Ferris wheel keeps turning, how many turns will it make in 4 minutes (240 seconds)?

23 cars
(remainder)

10. Cars are parked in the parking lot in rows. One row is filled with cars before another row is started. Each row holds 28 cars. If 163 cars are parked in the lot, how many cars are in the row that is not full?

Choosing the Operation
(pages 42–43)

Solve each problem. Visualize the action to decide which operation to use.

36 seats
_____

1. An airplane has 270 seats. If 234 seats are filled, how many seats are empty?

1,837 air miles
_____

2. The airplane flew 1,097 air miles from Miami to New York. Then it flew 740 air miles from New York to Chicago. What was the total length of the trip?

36 seats
_____

3. In the first-class section, there are 9 rows with 4 seats in each row. How many seats are in first class?

26 rows
_____

4. There are 234 seats in the coach section. There are 9 seats in each row in coach. How many rows are in the coach section?

32,000 feet
_____

5. The airplane was flying at an altitude of 36,000 feet. The pilot decreased the altitude by 4,000 feet. At what altitude was the airplane then flying?

1½ pieces of luggage
_____

6. The 234 passengers had 351 pieces of luggage. What was the average number of pieces of luggage per person?

about 240 tons
_____

7. An empty airplane weighs about 150 tons. If 90 tons of fuel and cargo are loaded on the plane, how much will it weigh?

¼ hour
_____

8. It took $2\frac{1}{2}$ hours to fly from Miami to New York. It took $2\frac{1}{4}$ hours to fly from New York to Chicago. How much longer was the flying time from Miami to New York than from New York to Chicago?

855 miles
_____

9. If the airplane traveled at an average speed of 570 miles per hour, how far did it travel in $1\frac{1}{2}$ hours?

$643.50
_____

10. It costs the airline about $2.75 for each meal served on the airplane. How much did it cost the airline to serve a meal to each of the 234 passengers?

Two-Operation Problems

(pages 44–45)

Solve each problem. Remember to follow the five problem solving steps for both the hidden question and the main question.

Pizza Haven							

Pizza	Small	Large	Salad Bar		Subs	Half	Whole
cheese	$5.20	$ 8.60	with meal	$2.50	Italian	$1.50	$2.40
1 extra item	6.00	9.70	without meal	3.25	ham and cheese	1.65	2.60
2 extra items	6.80	10.70			steak	1.95	3.10
deluxe	8.30	13.00					

$12.10 _____

1. Phil bought 4 whole Italian subs and 1 salad bar. How much did he spend?

$3.70 _____

2. Inez ordered 1 small deluxe pizza and 1 large deluxe pizza. How much change did she get from $25?

$21.50 _____

3. Marie and Beth ordered 5 large cheese pizzas. They split the bill evenly. How much did each one spend?

6 ounces _____

4. Adam makes pizzas at the Pizza Haven. He uses a total of 48 ounces of cheese to make 1 large cheese pizza and 6 small cheese pizzas. He uses 12 ounces for the large pizza. He uses the rest equally on the small pizzas. How much cheese does he put on each small pizza?

$1.75 _____

5. Steven bought 5 ham-and-cheese half subs. How much change did he receive from $10?

2 pizzas _____

6. There are 12 slices in a large pizza. There are 7 people in the Manzo family. Each person wants 3 slices of pizza. How many large pizzas should they order?

$0.80 _____

7. How much do you save by buying 1 whole steak sub rather than 2 half steak subs?

$10.35 _____

8. Jan has a coupon for $1.75 off the price of a large pizza. She buys 1 large pizza with 1 extra item and a whole Italian sub. How much does she spend?

44½ hours _____

9. Adam works at the Pizza Haven for $8\frac{1}{2}$ hours on Mondays, Tuesdays, and Thursdays. He works for $9\frac{1}{2}$ hours on Fridays and Saturdays. (He is off on Wednesdays and Sundays.) How many hours does he work in 1 week?

$0.75 _____

10. Frank ordered the salad bar and half an Italian sub. How much more did he pay than if he ordered only a salad bar?

Choosing a Sensible Answer
(pages 46–47)

For each question, circle the answer that is the most reasonable.

1. Chris is carpeting the dining room. How much carpeting is needed?
   (100 square feet)   100 feet
   10 square feet   10 feet

2. What is the height of a door?
   80 square feet   80 feet
   8 square feet   (8 feet)

3. What is the volume of a refrigerator?
   180 cubic feet   180 square feet
   (48 cubic feet)   48 square feet

4. What is the length along 1 wall in a bedroom?
   (12 feet)   120 feet
   1,200 feet   12,000 feet

5. How high is a kitchen counter?
   3.6 inches   (36 inches)
   3.6 yards   36 yards

6. How much does a refrigerator weigh?
   200 ounces   (200 pounds)
   20 ounces   20 pounds

7. How much water will a bathtub hold?
   4.5 gallons   (45 gallons)
   450 gallons   4,500 gallons

8. How far does Leon walk to school?
   1.5 inches   1.5 feet
   1.5 yards   (1.5 miles)

9. How much does $\frac{1}{2}$ cup of cottage cheese weigh?
   4 pounds   40 pounds
   (4 ounces)   40 ounces

10. About how many days old are you?
    50 days   500 days
    (5,000 days)   50,000 days

Checking Estimates and Computations

(pages 48–49)

Solve each problem. Show an estimated answer and a computed answer for each problem.

1. A 10-speed bike sells for $199.99 at the Bike Outlet. It is on sale for $49 off the regular price. What is the sale price of the bike?

   Estimated Answer: $150
   (200 − 50 = 150)

   Computed Answer: $150.99
   (199.99 − 49.00 = 150.99)

2. A handlebar bike-bag sells for $10.49. A saddle bike-bag sells for $4.99. How much more does the handlebar bike-bag cost?

   Estimated Answer: $5
   (10 − 5 = 5)

   Computed Answer: $5.50
   (10.49 − 4.99 = 5.50)

3. Reflectors are packaged in boxes of 12. Bev wants to order 60 reflectors. How many boxes should she order?

   Estimated Answer: 6 boxes
   (60 ÷ 10 = 6)

   Computed Answer: 5 boxes
   (60 ÷ 12 = 5)

4. Each hook on the display rack holds 8 packages of hand grips. There are 16 hooks on the rack. How many packages can be put on the rack?

   Estimated Answer: 150 packages
   (15 × 10 = 150)

   Computed Answer: 128 packages
   (16 × 8 = 128)

5. The Bike Outlet sells parking stands for bikes. Each stand holds 6 bikes. How many stands must be purchased to park 35 bikes?

   Estimated Answer: 6 stands
   (36 ÷ 6 = 6)

   Computed Answer: 6 stands
   (35 ÷ 6 = 5.8, round up)

6. Chris bought a 3-speed bike for $179.99 and a car-top bike carrier for $49.99. He got a $50.00 trade-in on his old bike. How much did he owe?

   Estimated Answer: $180
   (180 + 50 − 50 = 180)

   Computed Answer: $179.98
   (179.99 + 49.99 − 50.00 = 179.98)

7. Lisa bought a new rear wheel for $28.95 and two new tires for $7.49 each. What was her total cost for the wheel and tires?

   Estimated Answer: $44
   (30 + 2(7) = 44)

   Computed Answer: $43.93
   (28.95 + 2(7.49) = 43.93)

8. Al needs new wheels for his bike. A front wheel costs $32.99. A rear wheel costs $38.99. A set of wheels (1 front and 1 rear wheel) costs $64.99. How much does Al save if he buys the set?

   Estimated Answer: $5
   (30 + 40 = 70; 70 − 65 = 5)

   Computed Answer: $6.99
   (32.99 + 38.99 = 71.98; 71.98 − 64.99 = 6.99)

9. Ruth paid $28.98 for a speedometer and 2 matching tires. The speedometer cost $15.00. How much did each tire cost?

   Estimated Answer: $7.50
   (30 − 15 = 15; 15 ÷ 2 = 7½)

   Computed Answer: $6.99
   (28.98 − 15.00 = 13.98; 13.98 ÷ 2 = 6.99)

Making a Diagram

(pages 54–55)

Draw a diagram on a separate paper to help you solve each of these problems.

___16 fence posts___

1. Vince is going to put a fence around his garden. The garden is 12 feet on each side. If he puts fence posts 3 feet apart, how many fence posts will he need?

___13½ blocks___

2. Wanda lives $8\frac{1}{2}$ blocks from Jackie's apartment. She jogged for $2\frac{1}{2}$ blocks toward Jackie's apartment and remembered that she had left her watch at home. She jogged back, got her watch, and jogged to Jackie's. How far did Wanda jog in all?

___12 choices___

3. Terry lives in Adamsville. He plans a trip from Adamsville to Bakertown to Cedarport. He may travel from Adamsville to Bakertown by car, bus, or train. He may travel from Bakertown to Cedarport by car, plane, bus, or ship. How many different ways might Terry travel from Adamsville to Cedarport?

___36 plants___

4. Bess is making a triangular garden. She is putting 4 daisy plants and 3 petunia plants at each corner and 8 daisy plants along each side to form a border. How many daisy plants does she need in all?

___11.5 km___

5. Jim lives 6 kilometers from Burger Delight. Aaron lives 2.5 kilometers from Burger Delight. Jim starts at his house, rides his bike 1.5 kilometers and remembers that his wallet is at home. He rides back home for his wallet. Then he rides to Burger Delight. After he eats lunch, he rides to Aaron's. How far does Jim ride his bike in all?

___9 choices___

6. Jose may order a chicken sandwich, a peanut butter sandwich, or a tuna sandwich. He can have it on white bread, wheat bread, or rye bread. How many choices does Jose have?

___18 stakes___

7. The base of Sue's tent is 8 feet by 10 feet. If she puts a stake in the ground every 2 feet around the base of the tent, how many stakes does she need?

___16 choices___

8. Debbie is going to paint the outside of her house. She may paint the house white, tan, gray, or yellow. She may paint the trim brown, blue, rust, or black. How many choices does she have for color combinations?

___5th day___

9. A caterpillar is climbing up a 10-foot wall. Each day the caterpillar climbs upward 3 feet. Each night it slips back down 1 foot. It starts at the bottom of the wall and climbs straight up. On which day will it reach the top of the wall?

___21 blocks___

10. Brad walked east 6 blocks to the ice cream shop. He walked north $4\frac{1}{2}$ blocks to Phil's. They walked 6 blocks west to the park. Then Brad took the shortest route back to his own house. How far did Brad walk in all?

Making a Ratio Table

(pages 56–57)

Make ratio tables on a separate paper to help you solve these problems.

6 eggs

1. Rosa owns a bake shop. Her recipe for bran muffins calls for 2 eggs for every 3 cups of bran cereal. How many eggs should she use with 9 cups of bran cereal?

12 cups of bran cereal

2. How many cups of bran cereal does Rosa need to make bran muffins if she uses 8 eggs?

60 customers

3. Rosa waited on 15 customers in 2 hours. At this rate, how many customers will she wait on in 8 hours?

$2.60

4. Sourdough biscuits are 3 for 65 cents. How much do 1 dozen biscuits cost?

9 biscuits

5. Pete has $1.95. How many biscuits can he buy?

30 hours

6. Rosa works 5 hours for every 8 hours her shop is open. Rosa's shop is open 48 hours each week. How many hours a week does Rosa work?

20 loaves of wheat bread

7. Rosa makes 3 loaves of rye bread for every 5 loaves of wheat bread she makes. If she makes 12 loaves of rye bread, how many loaves of wheat bread will she make?

9 loaves of rye bread

8. How many loaves of rye bread does Rosa make if she makes 15 loaves of wheat bread?

16 loaves of bread

9. Rosa estimated that 4 out of every 5 customers who came into her shop bought a loaf of bread. If 20 customers came into the shop, how many loaves of bread did Rosa expect to sell?

20 johnnycakes

10. Two cups of corn meal are used for every 5 johnnycakes. If Rosa has 8 cups of corn meal, how many johnnycakes can she make?

Making an Organized List
(pages 58–59)

Make an organized list on a separate paper to help you solve each problem.

6 different 3-digit numbers

1. How many different 3-digit numbers can you make with the numerals 7, 8, and 9 if you can use each numeral only once?

27 different 3-digit numbers

2. How many different 3-digit numbers can you make with the numerals 7, 8, and 9 if you can use each numeral once, twice, or three times?

9 different 2-digit numbers

3. How many different 2-digit numbers can you make with the numerals 7, 8, and 9 if you can use each numeral either once or twice?

24 different 3-digit numbers

4. How many different 3-digit numbers can you make with the numerals 6, 7, 8, and 9 if you can use each numeral only once?

24 different ways

5. A red, a green, a blue, and a yellow flag are raised up a flagpole, one under the other. How many different ways are there to arrange the 4 flags?

10 games

6. Amy, Barb, Carol, Donna, and Eva will play in a tennis match. Each player will play each other player once. How many games will be played?

10 different choices

7. The library has 5 books about the planets. Mike wants to check out 2 books. How many choices does he have?

15 handshakes

8. There are 6 finalists in the spelling bee. Each finalist shakes hands with each of the other finalists. How many handshakes are there?

12 different ways

9. Earl has 4 books and 3 games. How many different ways may he lend 1 book and 1 game to his brother?

20 different combinations

10. The stationery shop has 5 different color markers and 4 different color pencils. How many different combinations of 1 marker and 1 pencil are there?

Diagram, Ratio Table, List
(pages 60–61)

On a separate paper, use a diagram, ratio table, or organized list to help you solve each problem.

8 different
combinations

1. Anna is making costumes for the class play. She may use red, green, blue, or yellow cloth. She may use silver or gold trim. How many different combinations does she have to choose from?

20 yards

2. Anna needs 5 yards of trim for every 2 costumes she makes. How many yards of trim does she need for 8 costumes?

24 different ways

3. Abe, Bob, Carl, and Dave ran in the track meet. One of them finished first, one finished second, one finished third, and one finished fourth. In how many different orders could the 4 boys have finished the race?

28 times

4. Abe finishes first in 2 out of 7 races. At this rate, how many races does he need to run in order to finish first 8 times?

13 blocks

5. Fred lives 5 blocks west of school. Ted lives 3 blocks east of school. Fred starts at his house, walks $2\frac{1}{2}$ blocks toward school, and remembers that he doesn't have his homework. He goes back home, gets his homework, and then walks to Ted's. How far does Fred walk in all?

12 different ways

6. There are apples, bananas, plums, and pears in the fruit bowl. There are bran, oatmeal, and corn muffins in the cabinet. How many different ways may you choose 1 piece of fruit and 1 muffin for dessert?

15 choices

7. Six people want to play in the singles table tennis tournament. How many different choices are there for the two people who play the first game?

45 times

8. A gear turns 9 times for each 2 turns of a wheel. How many times does the gear turn if the wheel makes 10 turns?

40 feet

9. Kelly is roller-skating across the floor in a straight line. She skates forward for 20 feet, backward for 10 feet, forward for 20 feet, backward for 10 feet, and forward for 20 feet. How many feet is it from the place where she starts to the place where she stops?

28 times

10. An ant is walking around the frame of a window that is 4 feet by 3 feet. The ant stops to rest every 6 inches. How many times does the ant stop to rest if it makes one complete trip around the frame?

Finding a Pattern
(pages 62–63)

Continue the pattern in each progression.

1. 2, 6, 10, 14, 18, __22__, __26__   (+4)

2. 100, 97, 94, 91, 88, __85__, __82__   (−3)

3. 5, 4, 10, 9, 15, 14, __20__, __19__   (−1, +6)

4. 0, 3, 9, 12, 36, __39__, __117__   (+3, ×3)

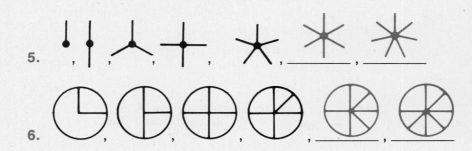

5.

6.

Find the patterns. Solve each problem.

$64

7. Sandy saved money to buy a camera. She saved $1 the first week, $2 the second week, $4 the third week, and so on. At this rate, how much did she save the seventh week?

48 minutes

8. The Film Club had a festival. The first film was 3 minutes long. The next film was 6 minutes. The third film was 12 minutes. If this pattern continued, how long was the fifth film?

$39

9. Liz would like to earn $3 the first week, $7 the second week, $11 the third week, $15 the fourth week, and so on. At this rate, how much would she be paid the tenth week?

65 minutes

10. Paulo has started an exercise program. He plans to exercise 5 minutes the first day, 15 minutes the second day, 25 minutes the third day, and so on. If this pattern continues, how many minutes will he exercise on the seventh day?

41 workers

11. The number of workers in the print shop changed from 57 in January to 53 in February to 49 in March. If this trend continued, how many workers were in the print shop in June?

8 times

12. Tom planted bushes that were 12 inches tall along a fence. Each time the bushes grew 3 inches, he trimmed off 2 inches. How many times did he trim the bushes before the bushes were 20 inches tall after a trimming?

Writing an Equation—Addition or Subtraction

(pages 64–65)

Write an equation on a separate paper to help you solve each problem.

475 people

($450 + n = 925$ or

$925 - 450 = n$)

1. The Youth Club had a street fair on Saturday and Sunday. On Saturday, 450 people came to the fair. If 925 people came to the fair in all, how many people were at the fair on Sunday?

120 plants

($67 + 53 = n$)

2. One booth sold plants. There were 67 plants sold on Saturday and 53 plants sold on Sunday. How many plants were sold in all?

38 plants

($67 - 29 = n$ or

$29 + n = 67$)

3. If 29 of the 67 plants sold on Saturday were hanging plants, how many were not hanging plants?

7 more cactus

($16 - 9 = n$)

4. Of the 53 plants sold on Sunday, 9 were ivy plants and 16 were cactus. How many more cactus than ivy plants were sold?

3½ hours

($2\frac{1}{2} + n = 6$)

5. Tom worked at the baseball toss booth and the snack bar. He worked at the fair for 6 hours in all. He worked at the baseball toss for $2\frac{1}{2}$ hours. How long did he work at the snack bar?

34 people

($43 - 9 = n$)

6. While Tom worked at the baseball toss, 43 people played the game. Only 9 people won prizes. How many people did not win prizes?

$4.75

($n + 1.50 = 6.25$)

7. Pete had $1.50 more to spend at the fair than Jill had. If Pete had $6.25, how much did Jill have?

3¼ hours

($1\frac{3}{4} + n = 5$)

8. Tanya spent $1\frac{3}{4}$ hours at the fair on Saturday. How many hours did she spend at the fair on Sunday if she spent 5 hours at the fair in all?

$1.30

($.85 + .45 = n$)

9. The snack bar sold hot dogs for $0.85. Hamburgers cost $0.45 more than hot dogs. How much did hamburgers cost?

$1.05

10. Tacos cost $0.25 less than hamburgers. How much did tacos cost? (Use the facts from Problem 9.)

Writing an Equation—Multiplication or Division

(pages 66–67)

Write an equation on a separate paper to help you solve each problem.

<u>45 people</u>
$(3 \times 15 = n)$

1. The street fair had 15 game booths with 3 people working at each booth. How many people were working at the game booths?

<u>8 balloons</u>
$(120 \div 15 = n)$

2. There are 120 balloons to decorate the 15 game booths. If the same number of balloons are used in each booth, how many balloons does each booth have?

<u>29 people</u>
$(87 \div 3 = n)$

3. On Saturday morning, the dart toss was played 87 times. Each person played 3 times. How many people played the dart toss game?

<u>7½ hours</u>
$(2\frac{1}{2} \times 3 = n)$

4. Anna worked at the dunking booth for $2\frac{1}{2}$ hours on Saturday. On Sunday, she worked 3 times as long as she did on Saturday. How long did she work on Sunday?

<u>23 books</u>
$(115 \div 5 = n)$

5. At the used-book booth, 115 books are displayed on 5 shelves. What is the average number of books per shelf?

<u>$6.25</u>
$(5 \times 1.25 = n)$

6. Matt, Paul, and Marcy each bought a book at the fair. Matt paid $1.25 for his book. Paul paid 5 times as much as Matt did for his book. How much was Paul's book?

<u>$0.25</u>
$(5 \times n = 1.25)$

7. Matt's book cost 5 times as much as Marcy's book. How much did Marcy's book cost?

Fresh-Squeezed Orange Juice

large glass $ .75
small glass $ .50

<u>27 large glasses</u>
$(4 \times n = 108)$

8. Orange juice was sold at the fair. There were 4 times as many small glasses as large glasses sold. If 108 small glasses were sold, how many large glasses were sold?

<u>$20.25</u>
$(.75 \times 27 = n)$

9. How much money was made on the sale of large glasses of orange juice? (Use the facts in Problem 8.)

<u>$74.25</u>
$(.50 \times 108 = n = 54;$
$20.25 + 54 = y)$

10. How much money was made on the sale of both large and small glasses of orange juice? (Use the facts in Problems 8 and 9.)

Writing Equations
(pages 68–69)

Write an equation on a separate paper to help you solve each problem.

315 cards
$(63 \times 5 = n)$

1. Jason has 63 baseball cards. Nathan has 5 times as many cards as Jason has. How many cards does Nathan have?

35 problems
$(29 + 6 = n)$

2. On his math test, Franco got 29 problems correct and 6 problems wrong. How many problems were on the math test?

471 red chairs
$(n - 27 = 444)$

3. There are 27 more red chairs than blue chairs in the lunchroom. If there are 444 blue chairs, how many red chairs are there?

61 teachers
$(915 \div 15 = n)$

4. There are 15 times as many students as teachers at Jefferson Junior High. There are 915 students. How many teachers are there?

4 kilometers
$(2.2 + 1.8 = n)$

5. Lara jogged 2.2 kilometers around the park. Angie jogged 1.8 kilometers farther than Lara. How far did Angie jog?

$47.25
$(189 \div 4 = n)$

6. Ms. Brimer spent $189 for four new tires for her car. How much did each tire cost?

$32.75
$(2 \times n = 65.50)$

7. This week, Anna's grocery bill was half what it was last week. She spent $65.50 last week. How much did she spend this week?

$8\frac{3}{4}$ yards
$(n - 6\frac{1}{2} = 2\frac{1}{4})$

8. Nell bought some ribbon to decorate a costume. She used $6\frac{1}{2}$ yards for the costume. She had $2\frac{1}{4}$ yards of ribbon left. How many yards of ribbon did she buy?

$\frac{3}{4}$ hour
$(3 \times n = 2\frac{1}{2})$

9. Dawn practiced the piano 3 times as long on Tuesday as she did on Monday. She practiced for $2\frac{1}{4}$ hours on Tuesday. How long did she practice on Monday?

$\frac{3}{4}$ hour
$(n + 1\frac{1}{4} = 2)$

10. Brad had science and math homework. He spent $1\frac{1}{4}$ more hours on his science homework than his math homework. If he spent 2 hours on science homework, how long did he spend on math homework?

Using a Formula
(pages 70–71)

Use the formulas listed on page 70 or in the Appendix on page 122 to help you solve these problems. Use 3.14 for π.

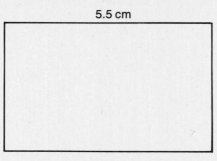

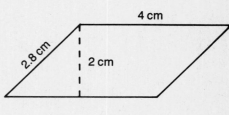

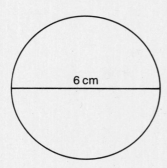

Find the areas of the figures above.

1. triangle ___32.5 cm²___   3. parallelogram ___8 cm²___

2. rectangle ___19.25 cm²___   4. circle ___28.26 cm²___

Find the perimeters of these figures shown above.

5. rectangle ___18 cm___   6. parallelogram ___13.6 cm___

___18.84 cm___

7. Find the circumference of the circle shown above.

___5 meters___

8. Jan fenced in a circular pen for her dog. The circumference of the pen was 15.7 meters. What was the diameter of the pen?

___9 feet___

9. The area of a rug is 108 square feet. It is 12 feet long. How wide is the rug?

___15 inches___

10. The area of a bird cage floor is 150 square inches. The floor is 10 inches wide. What is the length of the floor?

___144 square feet___

11. Melvin is planting a vegetable garden. The garden is 12 feet on each side. What is the area of the garden?

___314 square meters___

12. A water sprinkler shoots water a distance of 10 meters to water a circular region. What is the area of the region it waters?

Making a Hard Problem Easier
(pages 72–73)

Solve these problems. It may help you to think about similar but simpler problems.

12 min. 46 sec.

1. Dave fouled out of a basketball game with only 2 minutes 14 seconds left in the fourth quarter. Each quarter of the game was 15 minutes long. How many minutes of the fourth quarter had already been played?

3½ times

2. Kate played the guitar for $24\frac{1}{2}$ minutes. Wendy played the flute for 7 minutes. How many times longer did Kate play than Wendy?

$888.03

3. The school bought 27 new game jerseys for the football team. The jerseys cost $32.89 each. How much did the new game jerseys cost?

14.92 seconds

4. Four members of the relay team ran the 400-meter relays in 59.68 seconds. What was the average time for each runner?

5 tapes

5. Don has $23.89. Cassette tapes are on sale for $4.49. How many tapes can Don buy?

$64.84

6. Electricity costs an average of $0.0747 for each kilowatt hour used. The Wilsons used 868 kilowatt hours last month. What was their electric bill?

$6.96

7. Karen went shopping and spent $27.84. This was 4 times what Marie spent. How much did Marie spend?

$12.34

8. You have $37.02. You want to put twice as much in the bank as you spend. How much can you spend?

1 foot 5 inches

9. A piece of lumber is 7 feet 3 inches long. You cut off one board that is 2 feet 6 inches long. You cut off another board that is 3 feet 4 inches long. How much of the original board is left?

$0.75

10. Jon bought a 1.65-pound package of ground meat for $2.97 and a 7.92-pound package of chicken. The package of chicken cost twice as much as the package of ground meat. How much per pound was the chicken?

Guessing and Checking

(pages 74–75)

Use the guess-and-check strategy to solve each problem.

13 and 15

1. The product of two numbers is 195. The difference between the two numbers is 2. What are the two numbers?

20 and 6

2. The sum of two numbers is 26. The product of the two numbers is 120. What are the two numbers?

456

3. A number has three digits. The three digits are consecutive. The sum of the digits is 15. The number is less than 500. What is the number?

5 dimes; 9 quarters

4. Carol has $2.75 in dimes and quarters. She has 14 coins in all. How many dimes and how many quarters does she have?

15 one-dollar bills; 17 five-dollar bills

5. Barbara has $100 in one-dollar bills and five-dollar bills. She has 2 more five-dollar bills than one-dollar bills. How many of each does she have?

sweater—$16.50; jacket—$21.50

6. A jacket and a sweater cost $38. The jacket costs $5 more than the sweater. How much does each cost?

5 22-cent stamps; 8 14-cent stamps

7. Mark bought some 14-cent stamps and some 22-cent stamps. He paid $2.22 for 13 stamps. How many of each kind did he buy?

48 years old

8. Mrs. Bell is twice as old as her daughter. The sum of their ages is 72. How old is Mrs. Bell?

5 dogs, 10 cats, 15 rabbits

9. The pet shop has 3 times as many rabbits as dogs. There are twice as many cats as dogs. There are 30 animals in all. How many of each animal are in the shop?

Art—8 shirts; Brad—9 shirts; Cary—12 shirts

10. Art, Brad, and Cary have 29 shirts in all. Cary has 4 more than Art. Brad has 1 more than Art. How many shirts does each one have?

3, 5, and 7 photographs

11. Altogether there were 15 photographs in the first three editions of the newspaper. The second edition had 2 more photographs than the first edition. The third edition had 2 more photographs than the second edition. How many photographs were in each edition of the newspaper?

Exact or Estimated Answers

(pages 76–77)

For each problem, first decide whether an exact or an estimated answer is necessary. Then solve the problem.

$40.00
(exact)

1. Ms. Carr wrote a check to pay for 2 sweaters and 1 shirt. The sweaters cost $12.25 each. The shirt cost $15.50. What was the amount of Ms. Carr's check?

no
(estimated)

2. Todd has $20. He wants to buy a shirt for $7.79 and a jacket for $13.95. Does he have enough money?

$1.64
(exact)

3. Megan bought 3 apples for $0.15 each and 1 pound of grapes for $1.19. She gave the clerk the correct amount of money. How much did she give the clerk?

yes
(estimated)

4. Glen's new library book has 248 pages. He wants to finish reading the book in 5 days. If he reads 55 pages a day, will he finish the book?

about 160 square feet
(estimated)

5. There are 4 windows in the classroom. Each window is 4 feet 10 inches wide and 8 feet 4 inches high. About how many square feet of glass are in the classroom?

1¾ hours
(exact)

6. Julie wants to practice the piano for 5 hours before her recital. She practices for $1\frac{1}{4}$ hours on Monday, $1\frac{1}{4}$ hours on Tuesday, and $\frac{3}{4}$ hour on Wednesday. How many more hours does she need to practice?

no
(estimated)

7. Jay counts calories and exercises to lose weight. His diet has no more than 2,000 calories per day. He eats a 689-calorie breakfast, a 515-calorie lunch, and a 794-calorie dinner. May he have a 175-calorie after-dinner snack?

$1.40
(exact)

8. James bought 10 22-cent stamps and 10 14-cent stamps. How much change did he get from $5.00?

no
(estimated)

9. Terri's baseball card album holds 500 cards. She has 279 cards. She buys 98 new cards. Her brother gives her 45 cards. Does she have enough cards to fill the album?

about 70 miles
(estimated)

10. Anne drives 6.83 miles one way to work each day. About how many miles does she drive to and from work during a 5-day work week?

More Than One Strategy

(pages 78–79)

Use whatever strategy works best for you to solve each problem.

1. Adam has dimes and quarters in his pocket. He has 11 coins with a money value of $1.85. How many of each coin does he have?

2. The bookstore sells 3 pencils for $0.50. How much do 1 dozen pencils cost?

3. The bookstore has blue pens, red pens, and black pens. It has yellow markers, green markers, red markers, and blue markers. How many different combinations of 1 pen and 1 marker are there?

4. Ruth spent 10 minutes doing homework on Monday, twice as long doing homework on Tuesday, and so on, doubling the length of time each day. If this pattern continued, how long did she spend doing homework on Friday?

5. How many feet of ribbon are needed to trim a rectangular tablecloth that is 5 feet 4 inches wide by 7 feet 2 inches long?

6. During practice, Kerrie ran the 100-meter dash in 20.65 seconds. At the track meet, she ran this same distance in 19.98 seconds. By how much did she improve her time?

7. Kyle, Jill, Matt, and Nellie are swimming in a relay. How many different arrangements are there for them to swim first, second, third, and fourth in the relay?

8. Carmen has 9 more books than Julie has. Together they have 29 books. How many books does Julie have?

9. The Bike Outlet paid $866.53 for 7 3-speed, 26-inch bikes. They sold the bikes for $189.99 each. What was their profit on the sale of these bikes?

10. Jean uses 20 meters of fencing to make a triangular pen for her rabbit. One side of the pen is 7.5 meters long. Another side of the pen is 6.2 meters long. How long is the third side?

Whole-Book Review

Read and reread each word problem. Then follow the directions to show your solution to the problem.

Teacher Note: Accept variations in students' plans as long as the plans yield correct answers.

1. Kurt is saving money. He has decided to save $1 the first week, $2 the second week, $4 the third week, $8 the fourth week, and so on. At this rate, how much will Kurt save the seventh week?

   a. Underline the question.
   b. Circle the needed facts in the problem.
   c. Describe your plan: Find a pattern.

   d. If an estimate can be made, show it here: cannot be made
   e. Carry out your plan. Answer: $64
   f. Check your answer. If you got an incorrect answer, tell how you know it is wrong. Then write the correct answer.
      Students who got incorrect answers should mention computation error or that the answer was not reasonable.

2. Together, Jean and Les wrote 21 programs for the computer club. Jean wrote 5 more programs than Les. How many programs did Jean write?
   a. Underline the question.
   b. Circle the needed facts in the problem.
   c. Describe your plan: Guess and check.

   d. If an estimate can be made, show it here: cannot be made
   e. Carry out your plan. Answer: 13 programs
   f. Check your answer. If you got an incorrect answer, tell how you know it is wrong. Then write the correct answer.
      Students who got incorrect answers should mention computation error or that the answer was not reasonable.

3. Kelly is making a (hexagonal) (six-sided) flower garden. To form a border for the garden, she is putting (3 rose bushes at each corner) and (6 rose bushes along each side). How many rose bushes does Kelly need?

   a. Underline the question.

   b. Circle the needed facts in the problem.

   c. Describe your plan: ___Make a diagram, then count.___

   _____

   d. If an estimate can be made, show it here: ___cannot be made___

   e. Carry out your plan. Answer: ___54 rose bushes___

   f. Check your answer. If you got an incorrect answer, tell how you know it is wrong. Then write the correct answer.

   ___Students who got incorrect answers should mention computation error or___

   ___that the answer was not reasonable.___

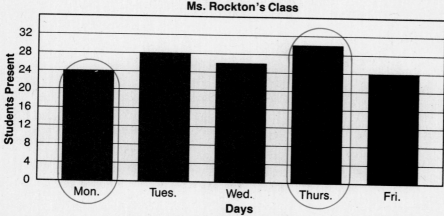

Ms. Rockton's Class

4. How many more students were in Ms. Rockton's class on Thursday than on Monday?

   a. Underline the question.

   b. Circle the needed facts in the problem.

   c. Describe your plan: ___Subtract (students present on Thursday – students___

   ___present on Monday = how many more students present on Thursday)___

   d. If an estimate can be made, show it here: ___cannot be made___

   e. Carry out your plan. Answer: ___6 more students___   (30 – 24 = 6)

   f. Check your answer. If you got an incorrect answer, tell how you know it is wrong. Then write the correct answer.

   ___Students who got incorrect answers should mention computation error or___

   ___that the answer was not reasonable.___

Go on to the next page.

Whole-Book Review (Continued)

5. Karl and Kim have part-time jobs. Last month, Karl worked (51 hours) That was (3 times) as many hours as Kim worked. <u>How many hours did Kim work?</u>
   a. Underline the question.
   b. Circle the needed facts in the problem.

   c. Describe your plan: _Write an equation. Let n = number of hours Kim_
      worked; 51 = 3n.

   d. If an estimate can be made, show it here: _cannot be made_

   e. Carry out your plan. Answer: _17 hours_

   f. Check your answer. If you got an incorrect answer, tell how you know it is wrong. Then write the correct answer.

      Students who got incorrect answers should mention computation error or

      that the answer was not reasonable.

6. Ashley bought a new guitar for ($250) She paid ($82 down) and agreed to pay the balance in (6 equal payments) <u>How much did Ashley pay each month?</u>
   a. Underline the question.
   b. Circle the needed facts in the problem.

   c. Describe your plan: _Two operations: subtract and divide_

   d. If an estimate can be made, show it here: _cannot be made_

   e. Carry out your plan. Answer: _$28_   _(250 − 82 = 168; 168 ÷ 6 = 28)_

   f. Check your answer. If you got an incorrect answer, tell how you know it is wrong. Then write the correct answer.

      Students who got incorrect answers should mention computation error or

      that the answer was not reasonable.

Appendix

Table of Measures

Metric System		Customary System

Length

Metric System	Customary System
10 millimeters (mm) = 1 centimeter (cm)	12 inches (in.) = 1 foot (ft.)
10 centimeters 100 millimeters } = 1 decimeter (dm)	3 feet 36 inches } = 1 yard (yd.)
10 decimeters 100 centimeters } = 1 meter (m)	1,760 yards 5,280 feet } = 1 mile (mi.)
1,000 meters = 1 kilometer (km)	6,076 feet = 1 nautical mile

Area

Metric System	Customary System
100 square millimeters (mm²) = 1 square centimeter (cm²)	144 square inches (sq. in.) = 1 square foot (sq. ft.)
10,000 square centimeters = 1 square meter (m²)	9 square feet = 1 square yard (sq. yd.)
100 square meters = 1 are (a)	4,840 square yards = 1 acre (A.)
10,000 square meters = 1 hectare (ha)	640 acres = 1 square mile (sq. mi.)

Volume

Metric System	Customary System
1,000 cubic millimeters (mm³) = 1 cubic centimeter (cm³)	1,728 cubic inches (cu. in.) = 1 cubic foot (cu. ft.)
1,000 cubic centimeters = 1 cubic decimeter (dm³)	27 cubic feet = 1 cubic yard (cu. yd.)
1,000,000 cubic centimeters = 1 cubic meter (m³)	

Mass/Weight

Metric System	Customary System
1,000 milligrams (mg) = 1 gram (g)	16 ounces (oz.) = 1 pound (lb.)
1,000 grams = 1 kilogram (kg)	2,000 pounds = 1 ton (T.)
1,000 kilograms = 1 metric ton (t)	

Capacity

Metric System	Customary System
1,000 milliliters (mL) = 1 liter (L)	8 fluid ounces (fl. oz.) = 1 cup (c.)
	2 cups = 1 pint (pt.)
	2 pints = 1 quart (qt.)
	4 quarts = 1 gallon (gal.)

Time

60 seconds = 1 minute	365 days }		
60 minutes = 1 hour	52 weeks } = 1 year		
24 hours = 1 day	12 months }		
7 days = 1 week	366 days = 1 leap year		

Operations Chart

Action	Operation
Joining different-sized groups (a different number in each group) to find a total	Addition
Separating Objects to find a group that is left or **Comparing two groups** to find the difference	Subtraction
Joining equal groups to find a total	Multiplication
Sharing equally to find the size of each group or **Making groups of a given size** to find the number of groups	Division

Geometric Formulas

Perimeter (P)
(the distance around a figure)

square $\qquad P = 4s$
rectangle $\qquad P = 2l + 2w$

Circumference (C)
(the distance around a circle)

circle $\qquad C = \pi d$
$\qquad$ or $\quad C = 2\pi r$

Area (A)
(the number of square units enclosed by the figure)

square $\qquad A = s^2$
rectangle $\qquad A = lw$
parallelogram $\quad A = bh$
triangle $\qquad A = \frac{1}{2}bh$
circle $\qquad A = \pi r^2$

Note: $\pi = \frac{22}{7}$ or 3.14

square

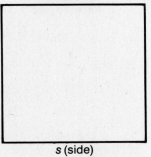

s (side)

rectangle

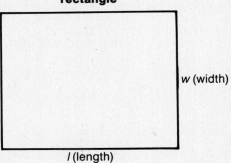

w (width)

l (length)

triangle

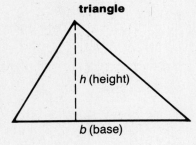

h (height)

b (base)

parallelogram

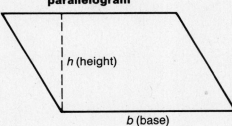

h (height)

b (base)

circle

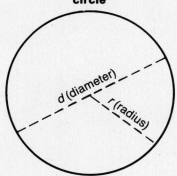

d (diameter)

r (radius)